THE ART OF FINE
TOOLS

written and photographed by
Sandor Nagyszalanczy

The Taunton Press

Cover photo: Courtesy Lee Valley Tools

Taunton
BOOKS & VIDEOS
for fellow enthusiasts

Printed in the United States of America
10 9 8 7 6 5 4 3 2 1

The Taunton Press, 63 South Main Street, PO Box 5506, Newtown, CT 06470-5506
e-mail: tp@taunton.com

Distributed by Publishers Group West

Library of Congress Cataloging-in Publication Data

Nagyszalanczy, Sandor.
    The art of fine tools / Sandor Nagyszalanczy.
        p.   cm.
    ISBN 1-56158-263-8
    1. Woodworking tools. I. Title.
TT186.N335 1998
684'.08.'028—dc21   98-6562
                                                              CIP

*To the unknown and anonymous craftsmen
who made many of the remarkable and artistic
woodworking tools in this book*

A C K N O W L E D G M E N T S

I'd like to thank all the individuals who allowed me to photograph their magnificent tool collections: Al Anderson, Fred Armbruster, Michael Armstrong, Curtis Bowden, Dan Comerford, Fred Damsen and The Japan Woodworker Catalog, Martin J. Donnelly Antique Tools in Bath, N. Y., Allan Foster, George Gaspari, Paul Hamler, Steve Johnson, Frank Kosmerl, David Kretchun, Patrick and Lisa Leach, Albert LeCoff, Mel Miller, Eric M. Peterson, Valdis Petersons, Bill S. Phillips, Roger B. Phillips, Wm. R. Robertson, Roberto Rodriguez and the American Precision Museum in Windsor, Vt., the Toolz Company of Palo Alto, Calif., Clifford R. Sapienza, Darrell Six, Roger K. Smith, Bud Steere, and Jon Zimmers Antique Tools of Portland, Ore. Without their hospitality and kind assistance, this book would be very empty and sad-looking indeed.

Extra-special thanks go to the following individuals, whose help far exceeded the call of duty: Steven F. Dice and the Pacific Northwest Tool Collectors, Leonard Lee and Lee Valley Tools, Ronald W. Pearson, D.O., Don Rosebrook, and John and Janet Wells.

For their technical assistance and contacts, I am grateful to Ken Bassett, Doug Cunningham, Roger Heitzman, Lester Markarian, Johannes Michelsen, Toshio Odate, Bill Rigler and the Mid-West Tool Collectors Association, Erv Shaffer, and I Made Suryasa. For their photographic assistance, thanks go to Michael Dresdner, Ann Gibb, and Ninette Maumus; to Ray Pilon and Sarah Dunn at Lee Valley Tools; and to Drew Strizik and the crew at Bay Photo Lab.

Finally, I'd like to express my appreciation to the folks at The Taunton Press who were directly responsible for producing this book, including publisher Jim Childs, associate publisher Helen Albert, text editor Ruth Dobsevage, art director Jodie Delohery, managing editor Carolyn Mandarano, designer and layout artist Mary Terrizzi, and publishing assistant Joanne Renna.

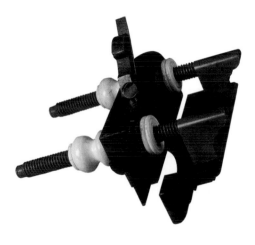

CONTENTS

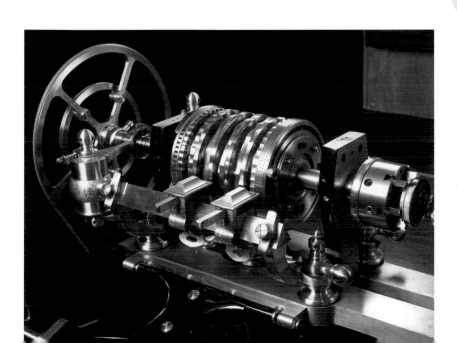

A well-made tool is a thing of beauty that's as much of a pleasure to look at as it is to use. But to enjoy lovely tools, one doesn't have to run out to the shop and raise a shaving or kick up a cloud of sawdust. Sometimes, it's enough just to sit back and gaze with admiration. The figured-rosewood and brass body of a try square, the fancy Victorian pattern cast into the handle of an antique scraper, the intricate iron filigree decorating the base of a treadle-powered scrollsaw—elements such as these have the universal appeal of a work of fine art.

You don't have to be a woodworker or know anything about tools to appreciate their inherent beauty, but attractive tools have an extra-special meaning to people who work with wood: I have a hunch that they are at least part of what inspired them to take up the craft in the first place. Visit any woodworking supply fair or antique-tool auction and you'll see the aisles filled with aspiring woodworkers coveting the hundreds of gorgeous hand and power tools on display. Fortunately, it's possible to enjoy an attractive, well-made tool, such as a fruitwood handplane or an engraved brass marking gauge, without having to buy it, just as most car enthusiasts who can't shell out megabucks for a vintage Ferrari can still admire its seductive bodywork or thrill to tales of its adrenaline-pumping performance.

This book is a celebration of the world's most incredible woodworking tools — tools of unique or unusual design that were crafted with remarkable precision, sumptuous materials, or artistic decoration. They deserve an intimate examination to appreciate fully their special qualities. On these pages you will discover tools that range in age from historic to modern, including a wide range of 19th-century carpentry and cabinetmaking tools and tools from Eastern and Western cultures. In addition to an extensive collection of hand tools, including saws, hammers, braces, chisels, layout tools, and planes, you will also find human-powered machines and tools that normally wouldn't be found in woodworking shops, such as miniatures and tools that embody more art than function. Most of these remarkable tools were gathered for personal collections, purchased from tool dealers and at auctions, flea markets, and estate sales across America and around the world. Many are rare pieces making their first public appearance.

Although tools that are as beautiful as they are functional are still being made today, many of the most interesting, intricate, and ornate tools come to us from the past. Older tools are like time capsules, with much to teach us about their makers' lives and style of work. Most simple tools were created out of necessity, shaped like a bird's wing and a handle fashioned to fit the hand. Some of the basic forms have survived for centuries essentially unchanged. Tools that are staples of the carpenter's chest, such as the hammer and handsaw, have remained the same in form and construction since the time of the ancient Romans.

While many people may appreciate the beauty of the ornate tools featured in these pages, woodworkers may be suspicious of the utility of highly adorned tools—were they made more for show than for making shavings? You may be surprised to learn that all but a handful of the "art" tools (which are featured at the end of the book) were, in their time, used daily. Many of the wooden tools show a tremendous amount of wear, and even user-made repairs, often visible in the photographs. And if you're upset by the fact that most of these tools now occupy display cabinets instead of tool chests, please remember that they are valuable heirlooms, delicate and irreplaceable. As romantic a wish as it is that we keep such tools as "daily users," it's more appropriate for them to be retired with dignity and kept in a place of honor. While we may remain envious of those with the time and means of finding and buying such tools, I think we owe a certain debt to the perseverance of the collectors who restore, preserve, and protect these precious artifacts and, ultimately, the rich history of woodworking that goes with them.

Whatever your background, it is the goal of this book to acquaint you with tools you may never get a chance to see in person, much less use, since many are locked away in the vaults of large private collections. The photographs provide an intimate portrait of these treasures; the accompanying text describes their origins and makers, and in some cases explains construction details and methods of use. These intriguing vignettes convey a sense of each tool's history, which is often colorful. Taken together, they stand as a tribute to human industry and aesthetics.

It is my hope that this book will cause you to look at woodworking tools a little differently. As this collection richly demonstrates, a tool can be far more than a utilitarian implement whose sole purpose is to perform a mundane task. When designed and wrought to high levels of craftsmanship, a tool transcends its function and becomes an object of art worthy of attention in its own right. If you're a woodworker, this book may inspire you to carve your initials on your best planes or perhaps build a few "special" tools of your own. A cherished tool adds immense pleasure to woodworking, and you will have an heirloom to pass on when your woodworking days are over.

MARKING AND MEASURING INSTRUMENTS

While making a pile of sawdust marks the progress of almost any woodworking project, it's the work that takes place ahead of the sawing, planing, boring, and pounding that often determines a project's success or failure. It doesn't much matter how attractive or precise the joinery is in a bookcase if it doesn't fit into the alcove it was built for.

Marking the length and shape of parts, miter and bevel angles, and joinery is part of the layout process that takes a design off a paper plan and turns it into a physical object. Now you *can* build just about anything without a ruler or yardstick using the "story stick method," where marks on a stick are used to represent the dimensions of all the parts. But unless you start with a full-sized drawing—which is impractical for a large piece such as a dining table—it's almost always easier to lay out a project by using rules, tape measures, or yardsticks. In fact, the ability to measure and lay down written records is one of the hallmarks of an organized society, and over the centuries, many different systems evolved (see the sidebar on p. 11).

The earliest rules used in the woodworking trades were as long as needed: a yard, a rod, etc. But it's a bit awkward to carry around a yardstick—or even a foot ruler—in your pocket. Hence, the development of the folding rule, an easy-to-carry a tool that will measure 12 in., 18 in., or 24 in. Some rules incorporated special scales for measuring scale drawings and plans or had slide-out end calipers for checking the thickness of boards or the dimensions of small parts. For even longer lengths, section "zig-developed. enced user such a rule 6-ft. part faster "zig zag" (this still popular in cans preferred a convenient form developed the suring tape in By the mid-1900s,

the multi-zag rule" was An experienced user can fold out and measure a than you can say style of rule is Europe). Americans longer and more of measure and wind-up mea-the mid-1800s. tape measures

existed in all sizes and styles, often with decorative pocket-sized cases that advertised products and patented design features to allow taking direct inside readings (see pp. 184-185).

But what if you have really long stock or curved parts to measure? You can always take a rule and flip it end for end to cover a long part, but inaccuracies can add up. Boat builders and lumber sawyers have long used a special tool called a "traveler" to handle such measuring and layout chores. A traveler is a wheel with increments of measure marked on the outer circumference. It can be wheeled down a log, sawn plank, or boat keel to get a surprisingly accurate reading of its length.

Laying out arcs, joinery to be cut, or the position of holes and hardware is an everyday event for most woodworkers. Tasks like these are made easier by tools such as marking gauges, trammel points, and calipers. Fancy or plain, an adjustable marking gauge can make mundane chores, such as laying out identical mortises on legs for a set of chairs, speedy and neat. If one setting is good, then a half-dozen might be even better, or so reasoned the maker of the gauge shown in the top photo on p. 19.

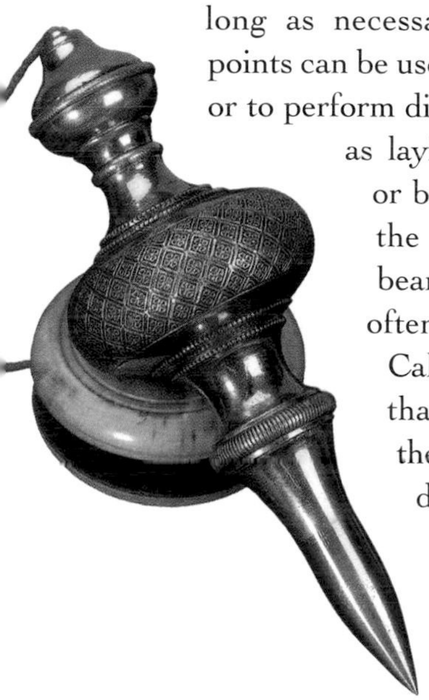

Mounted on a wood beam that's as long as necessary, a pair of trammel points can be used to mark a circle or arc or to perform division of segments, such as laying out a hexagonal form or bisecting an angle. Given the plainness of the wood beam, trammel points were often made very fancy. Calipers are another tool that can be plain, such as the blacksmith-forged tulip double calipers shown on p. 21, or elegant, such as the whimsical dancing-master calipers seen on pp. 20-21. Regardless of their style, calipers helped check the thickness of boards, as well as dimensioned parts and lathe turnings.

A tool that has changed little in centuries, but is nonetheless indispensable to the wood craftsman, is the square. The simplest so-called try squares are for just that: "trying" a frame or carcase corner to see if its members are square. All squares need to be sturdy to remain reliable, and hence square makers developed strong ways of locking the blade to the body that, to our delight, are also often decorative. The bevel gauge could be used for checking angles beyond 90°, and these tools were often decorative as well as handy.

In the building trades, carpenters used plumb bobs to make sure that the walls of a building were straight up and down. These simple weights on the end of a string, dangling free and aligned by the earth's gravity itself, show plumb reliably (except at a handful of mysterious spots on earth where gravity is supposed to be cockeyed!). Possibly due to their simplicity, plumb bobs have been created in an endless variety of shapes and sizes, from starkly plain to highly engraved (see pp. 34-35).

A slightly more sophisticated means of checking for plumb and level was developed early on by trapping a bubble of air in a curved clear glass vessel or vial filled with liquid mounted in a wood or metal body. Here again, gravity helps the bubble rise to the highest part of the arc, showing when the level is level. By mounting two or more bubble vials in a single body, you could check for plumb and level with a single tool. More clever yet, by making the vial's angle adjustable, the tool could be used to check for any angle between level and plumb. Such tools are called inclinometers, and carpenters used them to set the correct angle of rafters and to check the pitch of a roof.

Most of the basic marking and layout tools that the average woodworker is familiar with are plain, unadorned tools—the kind that you and I are likely to own and use on a daily basis. In this chapter, you'll get a look at some of the most remarkable and decorative versions of these tools ever made.

Silver layout and measuring tools

Among the fanciest layout tools in existence
is the heavily engraved pair of dividers at left,
which is inscribed "Belgrave Lodge, 1851."
The small square, just 3½ in. long,
is a Masonic presentation tool inscribed
"1929." The mechanical pencil, made by Otis
in about 1897, has a 4½-in. rule engraved
on it. The 12-in. folding rule at bottom
center has ivory inserts and an engraved
hinge. The rule to its right, also 12 in., has
mother-of-pearl inserts and a pull-out caliper.
Marked sterling, it was made by the
Gorham Company.

From the collection of Roger B. Phillips

Ivory rule with gilt frieze

Probably created for an exhibition or for special presentation, this 12-in.-long ivory rule features a frieze of mythological figures and fantastic creatures embossed into its gilt-covered copper center panel. Made in Europe in 1849, the rule bears a maker's mark and a small kite symbol. The rule's center panel (detail, top) shows a fanciful scene of male and female figures frolicking, playing musical instruments, and riding in a chariot as well as upon mythological creatures, such as the horse/serpent on the left.

From the collection of Steve Johnson

Ivory folding rules

In the 19th century, a lot of folding ivory rules were produced by both American and English makers, including E. A. Stearns, the Stanley Rule & Level Company, Rabone, Preston, and Stevens. Rules came in many different lengths and styles, and the best ones were made from ivory with German silver hinges and accents. Despite the color variations, all the rules shown at right are ivory; yellowing is a sign of use and age. Several of these rules incorporate a pull-out head that functions as a caliper. The cute little single-fold rule at center bottom has a flip-out penknife on one leg and a mechanical pencil on the other.

From the collection of Don Rosebrook

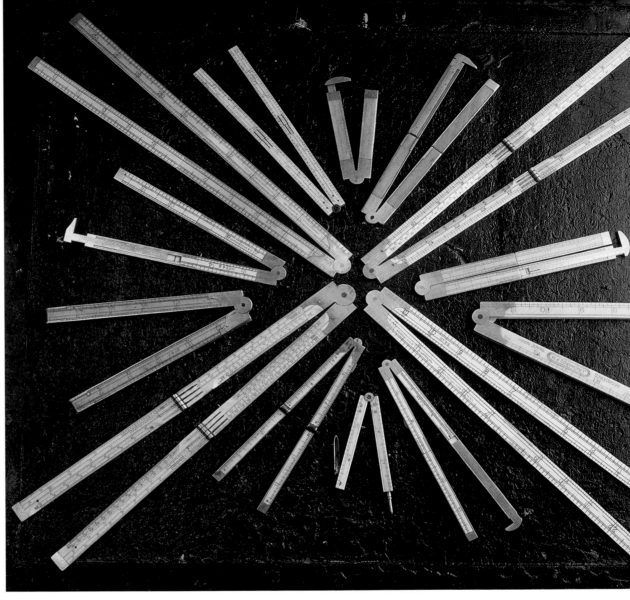

17th-century folding rule

Dated 1660, the boxwood 12-in. folding rule at left had many owners, as the stamps of several of them along its edges and back attest. James Burton (the name stamped on its decorated side) is likely the maker.

Allan Foster Collection

DIVIDING THE WORLD INTO MEASURED PARTS

I t's easy to pick up a yardstick made in Boston and a tape measure manufactured in San Francisco and not marvel at the fact that the divisions of inches and feet all match. But this hasn't always been the case.

Many different systems of measurement have been used over the past several thousand years. The oldest known measuring tools are attributed to the ancient Egyptians—one rule in the Cairo Museum is dated at 2600 B.C. The Egyptians made their rules primarily from stone or wood, using their own divisions of distance: the cubit, palm, and digit. Biblically derived, a cubit is about 1½ ft. in length. A palm divides the cubit into six parts, each about 3 in. long. Each palm is then divided into four digits.

By the birth of Christ, the Romans had developed a uniform system of measurement based on the human foot, and the system was used throughout their extensive empire. Unfortunately, this sensible approach was lost after the empire crumbled, and by the 18th and 19th centuries there were countless measurement standards in use in Europe alone. (The situation was even worse when it came to weight and volume measures. It is said that in every English market town, disreputable dealers had two bushels for weighing produce: a smaller one to use when selling, and a larger one to use when buying!)

Fortunately, today only two standards of measurement are in primary use throughout the world: the English system (inch, foot, and yard) and the metric system (millimeter, centimeter, and meter). When the English system was developed, lengths were based on the imperial standard yard, the prototype that defines a yard as the distance between two lines on a bronze bar made in 1845. Since the bar is shrinking by 1.5 millionths of an inch per year, the United States adopted its own copy in 1889, and has since redefined a yard as the length of the path traveled by light in a vacuum in $1/299{,}792{,}458$ of a second—how's that for accurate?

The metric system was developed in France in the 1790s. It defines a meter as one ten-millionth of the distance from the equator to the North Pole (with the line running through Paris, of course). The metric standard is in general use by the vast majority of countries worldwide (and all countries use it for scientific work). Most countries that still employ local systems of measurement have converted or are converting to the metric system.

Three fancy rules

Below right is a 24-in. brass and boxwood folding rule made by John Rabone & Sons, with a fancy pressed design on the hinge. In the middle is a 12-in. solid-brass ruler that is stamped "made in China." The back, shown here, has a fancy pressed design illustrating the myth of the dragons and the pearl. The rule's less ornate working side is inscribed "California Pacific Exhibition, San Diego 1935." The rule at left is a 24-in. brass folding rule, also made by Rabone, with fancy hinge overlays that are not only decorative, but also add strength.

From the collection of Roger B. Phillips

This tool-chest selection, from the Allan Foster Collection, exhibits not only the extensive variety of tape measures that have been manufactured, but also the evolution of the tape as a woodworking tool. One of the earliest manufacturers of metal and fabric retractable tapes, George M. Eddy of Brooklyn, New York, produced large, leather-cased tapes for carpenters as well as workers in other trades. In the 1880s, Eddy developed the handy metal-cased pocket tape, such as the three round metal cases at the center of the lid of the chest.

Another approach to the flexible, retractable metal tape is demonstrated by the Farrand Patent Rapid Rule, patented in 1922. Available in several models (shown at far right, inside the chest), the case was a storage container for the flexible metal tape, which came entirely out of the case for use. Farrand even produced a caseless model, with two clips that held the looped metal tape. Stanley bought Farrand's patent in the 1930s and developed its own version for the Four Square tool line (shown atop the tan Stanley Pull Push Rule box just right of center).

Just to its left are two later, more conventional Four Square tape models. Another tape that pulled all the way out of its case like the Farrand was the Donut, made by Lufkin. A number of other, later tape models by both Stanley and Lufkin are shown in the lid of the chest, including the colored Bakelite Stanley tapes and the Art Deco styled Lufkin Aristocrat tape, once a hardware-store give-away. Probably the oddest tape in the bunch is the chrome double-case-size Lufkin demolition tape (left of the Donut), which was designed specifically for calculating the size of a dynamite charge for destroying timber, concrete, and steel walls of various thicknesses!

Changing the shape of the pocket tape's case from round to D-shaped was a more recent improvement that allowed the user to take quicker inside measurements (and the tape didn't flop over when laid down). At the right side of the far back row are D-case tapes by Stanley, which have a window and pointer for reading an inside measurement directly, and by Master, including the locking Lumtape, which features a scale for calculating board feet of lumber.

British-American tape measure

This small brass-cased tape measure was made in commemoration of the famous London air lift, when food and supplies were sent from the United States to war-ravaged England at the end of World War II.

Allan Foster Collection

Lady's Man tape measure

The Lady's Man pocket tape measure, by the Master Rule Company, exploited a relatively new material: Bakelite plastic. The 6-ft. tape's durable orange case was set off nicely by the stylishly designed silver box it came in.

Courtesy of Jon Zimmers

Log caliper/traveler

Made by F. M. Greenleaf of Littleton, New Hampshire, this ingenious "walking" tool not only checked a log's length, but also calculated the number of board feet of lumber it contained. The length of a log was measured by means of the ten-spoked "walking wheel" mounted at the end of the tool. The tips of the spokes are 6 in. apart, so a complete revolution ticks off 5 ft. of length. To make starting and keeping track of measurements easier, one of the spokes had a lead weight (so it always was at the bottom, and hence started each measurement) and others had colored bands marking off feet. Once a log's length had been ascertained, the tool's enormous caliper was set to the log's diameter, which showed the number of board feet for logs of various lengths on a scale marked along the shaft of the tool. While the tool's design was clever, it was evidently inconvenient to carry around, as many loggers stripped the tools of their skin-piercing, spiked walking wheels!

From the collection of Steven F. Dice

Star traveler

Appearing to be a user-made tool, this traveler wheel has its 24-in. circumference divided into 1-in. increments. It appears to have been cast from brass and then turned smooth on a lathe. Travelers were especially handy for measuring the length of curved parts or the circumference of round forms. Wheelwrights used them to measure the rims of wooden wagon wheels when fitting metal tires.

Collection of Roger K. Smith

Folding steel traveler

Patented by C. W. Brackett in 1885, this traveler wheel folds small enough to fit in a pocket or pouch. Held at the center point, the thin steel device is rolled along a surface, starting at the zero mark etched on its 12-in. circumference. A secondary wheel geared to the large wheel (just ahead of this user's thumb) records the number of times the traveler rolls past the 12-in. mark, up to 12 ft.

From the collection of Patrick and Lisa Leach

Eagle marking gauge

Cabinetmakers often made their own panel gauges for laying out cuts on wide panels. Made from mahogany stained dark, the gauge shown here has a fence embellished with two carved eagles, each with piercing orange glass eyes.

Courtesy of Martin J. Donnelly Antique Tools, Bath, New York

Multiple marking gauge

Patented by Brown and Berry in 1868, this multiple marking gauge is probably one of the most elaborate marking gauges ever made. In addition to a regular mortising gauge, the tool has no fewer than five additional marking gauges. Thanks to sliding brass strips dovetailed into the rosewood body, four of these gauges are independently adjustable once the fence is set.

David Kretchun collection

Fancy marking gauges

Each made of a different material, these marking gauges represent some of the fanciest that were available to the 19th-century cabinetmaker. Each gauge has a flanged brass fence stock: (from left to right) ebony and brass, all brass with a tubular beam, ivory and brass. All three are mortising gauges, with two pins, one fixed and one adjustable for setting the width of a mortise.

From the collection of Roger B. Phillips

Commonly know as dancing-master calipers, many different legged calipers were shop made throughout the 18th and 19th and centuries and into the early 20th century. The calipers get their name from their shape, usually dancing legs, though some show entire silhouettes of ladies or men (and, occasionally, on a risqué example, both). Considered folk art, many dancing-master calipers show the whimsy of their maker: legs bare or stocking clad, female or male, elegant or awkward. Though the profiles on most calipers look best with the legs set to check inside dimensions, the legs can usually be rotated to take outside measurements as well.

The assortment shown here, from the collection of Ronald W. Pearson, D.O., represents the range of calipers that were made in the past 200 years. Note some of the details: the frilly garters and hose on the large pair at center top; the old-fashioned lace-up shoes on the copper calipers at bottom center; the pregnant female forms, right side, second from top. The oldest example in this assortment is the combination caliper/divider at center bottom (the ladies with pointed heads), and the newest is the pair of derby-clad men (left side, center), which is a reproduction of a vintage European tool.

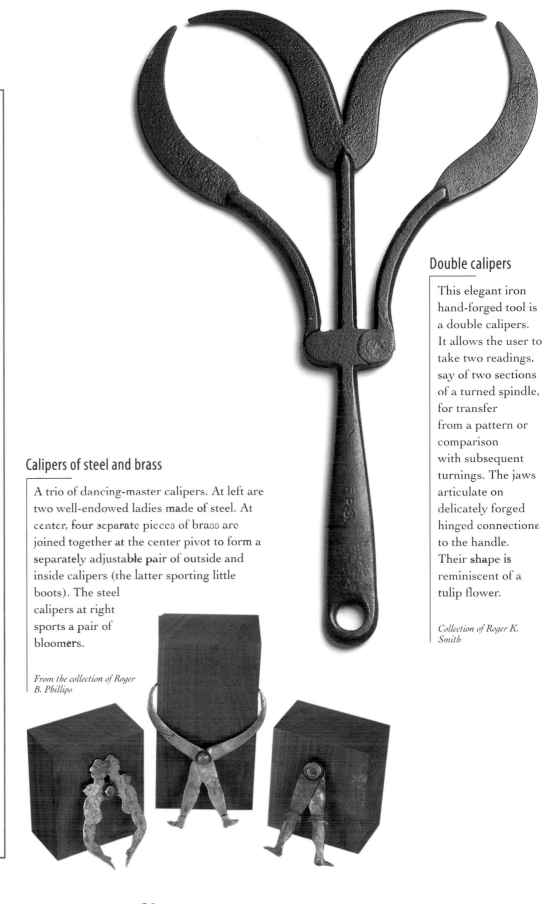

Calipers of steel and brass

A trio of dancing-master calipers. At left are two well-endowed ladies made of steel. At center, four separate pieces of brass are joined together at the center pivot to form a separately adjustable pair of outside and inside calipers (the latter sporting little boots). The steel calipers at right sports a pair of bloomers.

From the collection of Roger B. Phillips

Double calipers

This elegant iron hand-forged tool is a double calipers. It allows the user to take two readings, say of two sections of a turned spindle, for transfer from a pattern or comparison with subsequent turnings. The jaws articulate on delicately forged hinged connections to the handle. Their shape is reminiscent of a tulip flower.

Collection of Roger K. Smith

Try squares

Try squares are invaluable for checking the angle of two parts for square or striking a square line across a board. The squares in this group have blades that range from 3½ in. to 7½ in. The stocks, of rosewood or ebony, are fitted with a variety of brass escutcheons, which permanently secure their thin blades and in some cases identify their maker by their distinctive shapes.

From the collection of Steven F. Dice

Engraved brass framing square

This brass framing square was likely to have been fabricated by its user from thick sheet brass. Its 9-in.-long legs were then engraved with a lively geometric pattern.

Courtesy of Lee Valley Tools

Three try squares and an ebony dividers

The large try square at top has a 15-in.-long steel blade with the engraving "John Howarth Manufacturer Sheffield" surrounded by a faint floral pattern. This square has fancy brass escutcheons (that appear to be silver plated) inlaid into its ebony stock, which sports a small single-vial level. The other large square also has ornate brass escutcheons and a 12-in.-long blade. The small try square was made by Marples and Sons. The arms of the dividers, made of brass and ebony, are more than 16 in. long; their ends are fitted with steel tips.

From the collection of Roger B. Phillips

Two center-finding squares

Both of these squares have the decorative cast-iron bodies characteristic of tools made in the late 19th century. The larger Chaplin's Patent square, made by the Standard Tool Co., can be used as a square or a depth gauge; it has a center-finder head, which was also sold as part of a combo square set. The smaller tool, a Marshall's Patent universal square, was made by the Davis Level and Tool Company in the 1880s. Advertised as a combination tool, the Marshall not only worked as a center finder, but also was useful as a try square and depth gauge. The tool's 6-in. blade also pivots, making it a bevel gauge as well.

From the collection of Wm. R. Robertson

Bevel gauges

Angles are easily marked and measured with a good bevel gauge, and here are a few of the best. In front is a long user-made brass and rosewood shipbuilder's bevel. Small brass pins form the numbers and increments. At far left is a rosewood and brass Howard's Patent bevel. To its right is a much fancier Howard's Patent bevel, made around 1867. Its brass body has an ornate pattern cast into it, and even a small level vial along one edge. To its right is the same model with its reverse side out. At far right is a Rabone folding boxwood rule with a brass protractor scale.

From the collection of Don Rosebrook

Two combination tools

Frederich Ritchie's patented tool, shown at far right, was advertised at the time of its patent (1884) as "the complete tool for the woodworker." It features a square, a bevel gauge, a 6-in. graduated scale, and two levels. The tool, manufactured in Vanceborough, Maine, is made of ebony with nickel-plated brass fittings. For protection from job-site use, the two level vials have sliding covers. Not as versatile as the Ritchie, the rosewood and brass Hall & Knapp try square at right also has a built-in level in the handle.

David Kretchun collection

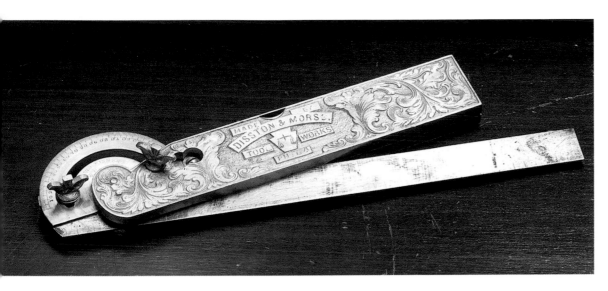

Disston presentation bevel square

Known primarily for his fine handsaws (see the sidebar on p. 99), Henry Disston also produced some excellent layout tools. Stamped "Disston & Morss," this richly detailed brass bevel gauge was patented by W. T. Fisher of Tennessee, who contracted with the company to manufacture the tool.

From the collection of Patrick and Lisa Leach

Ivory and ebony folding rule/bevels

These Stephens Company patented tools are more than just folding rules. Both 12-in. two-fold rules, patented in 1858, incorporate a bevel gauge, a protractor, and even a small level vial. At right, the No. 38 ivory rule; at far right, the No. 40 ebony rule.

David Kretchun collection

Brass and mahogany presentation level

Fancy brass escutcheons and wear plates were commonly added to vintage wood levels, both as decoration and as protection for the ends and edges. But few are as elaborate as this 30-in. level, made by J. M. Davidson of "Po'Keepsie," New York (town names marked on early tools often differ from their contemporary spellings; in this case Poughkeepsie). The tool, which was probably made in the late 1800s, has a main vial, two adjustable plumb vials, and also a sighting level. A peep sight atop the level focuses on a 45° mirror, which looks out of a hole in the end of the level. This allowed the level to be used as a builder's transit, say for leveling footings of a building that were many yards apart.

David Kretchun collection

Brass level with flip-down cover

The cover on this Van de Grift patent level flips down, to protect the alcohol-filled vial when it's not in use. Actually a small machinist's level, made by the Patent Level Co. of Bridgeport, Connecticut, this level comes in several variations, each with a different paint job and/or pierced pattern on the brass side wings.

From the collection of Valdis Petersons

French ivory and silver presentation level

This 6-in.-long carved ivory and engraved sterling-silver level reveals the maker's name: Canivet, a famous 18th-century French craftsman who had a workshop in Paris called "à la sphère." He made measurement instruments, including levels, although he was best known for his astronomical instruments, such as quadrants and telescopes.

From the collection of Roger B. Phillips

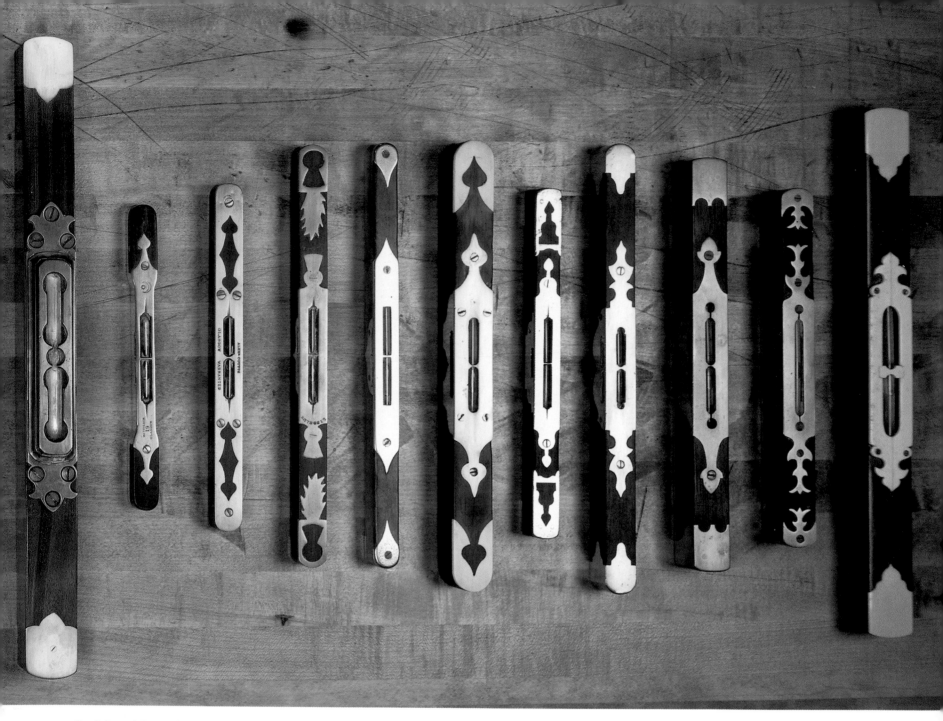

English and Scottish levels

Wooden levels made in the British Isles have a distinctive look and feature elaborate
variations in their brass, silver, or ivory wear plates. This collection of 11 levels includes
tools by John Fielding, of Sheffield, England; Dobic in Glasgow, Scotland; Alex Coutts,
of Glasgow; and Mathieson, of Glasgow. The bodies of the tools are made of ebony,
mahogany, ebonized mahogany, or bubinga.

From the collection of Roger B. Phillips

Melick inclinometer

With its ornate gold-painted details and engraved dial face, this Melick inclinometer was one of the most expensive levels of its day. It cost roughly 10 times what a typical wood level cost back in the late 19th century, when the Melick was made.

Courtesy of Jon Zimmers

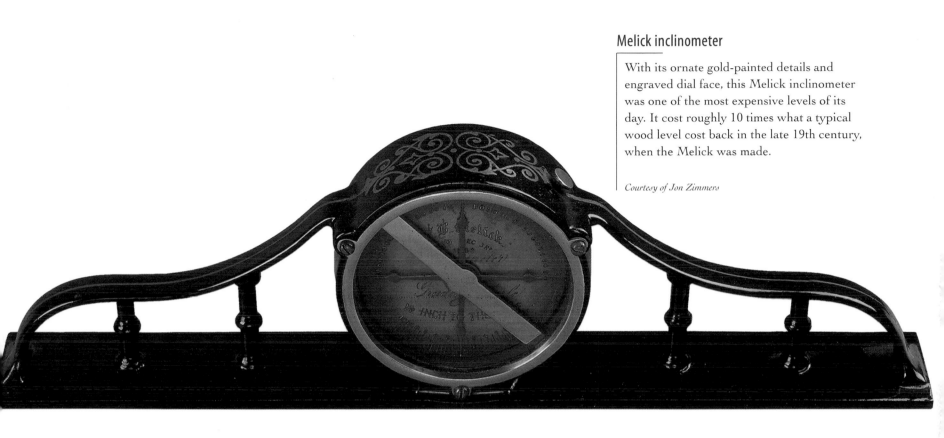

Davis & Cook , twin-vial and 90° aluminum levels

These levels were both patented around 1886. While most cast levels of this era were made of iron, Davis & Cook used aluminum for these cast levels. The rare twin-vial level at right is 18 in. long; the corner level at far right is 6¾ in. long.

Courtesy of Jon Zimmers

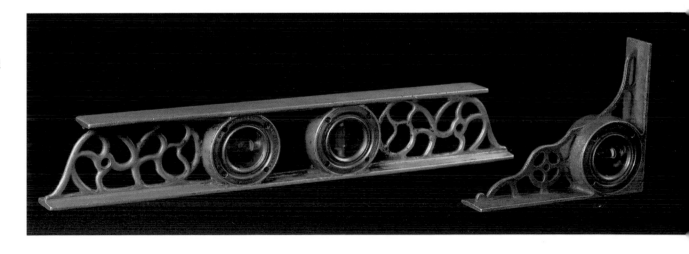

The latter half of the 19th century saw a surge in the manufacture of cast-iron levels. Sand-casting technology made it possible to incorporate ornate Victorian designs into the webbing between the level's rigid top and bottom surfaces. Because of the delicacy of some models, the examples we find today are often broken. L. Davis was a pioneer of this type of level, creating a series of ever more fanciful designs over a 25-year period. The most highly embellished examples of Davis' levels had bright-gold filigree accents (see the top photo on p. 32).

Among prominent makers of the day, only Davis was well known for producing basic levels and inclinometers in cast iron and wood. Whereas a basic level had one or more bubble vials rigidly mounted, an inclinometer typically had a single vial mounted in an adjustable circular protractor. By changing the setting, an inclinometer could check plumb or level or measure the angle of an inclined surface, such as a roof rafter or stair railing.

The cast-iron levels and inclinometers in the photo, from the collection of Don Rosebrook, represent the range of sizes, styles and types that were available to the woodworker in the late 19th century. Starting at the back row, these are: (left) a triple-vial 12-in. level by an unknown maker cast entirely from bronze; (center) a 7-in.

cast-iron inclinometer made by the Davis Level and Tool Co. after a 1867 patent; (right) an unusual 12-in. inclinometer with a geared adjustment mechanism operated by knobs extending on both sides. Once painted red and gold, the level has decorative engraving bearing the owner's initials and a date of 1877.

In the second row from the back: (left) a 12-in. inclinometer with very fine cast-iron filigree made by the Davis Level and Tool Co.; (center) a 6-in. level made c. 1910 by the Willamsburg Mfg. Co.; (right) A Webb's patent level, made by the Fitchburg Level Co. Its level vials are set in a common chamber filled with plaster.

In the third row from the back: (left and right) two models of pocket levels made after the 1850s, designed to be temporarily fastened to a straightedge or the blade of a square. The level at left is a Stanley iron No. 40 type 3. The brass-faced level at right was likely made by Chapin. At center, a Stanley No. 39 machinist's level type 1. This handy 6-in. level was used by craftsmen of many trades.

In the front row: (left) a 6-in. level by the Standard Tool Co.; (center) an 8-in. level with a paper label reading "Empire Spirit Level, Greene, Tweed & Co., N.Y." that employs the Webb patent used by the Fitchburg Level Co.; (right) a 6-in. three-vial level made by the Davis Level and Tool Co.

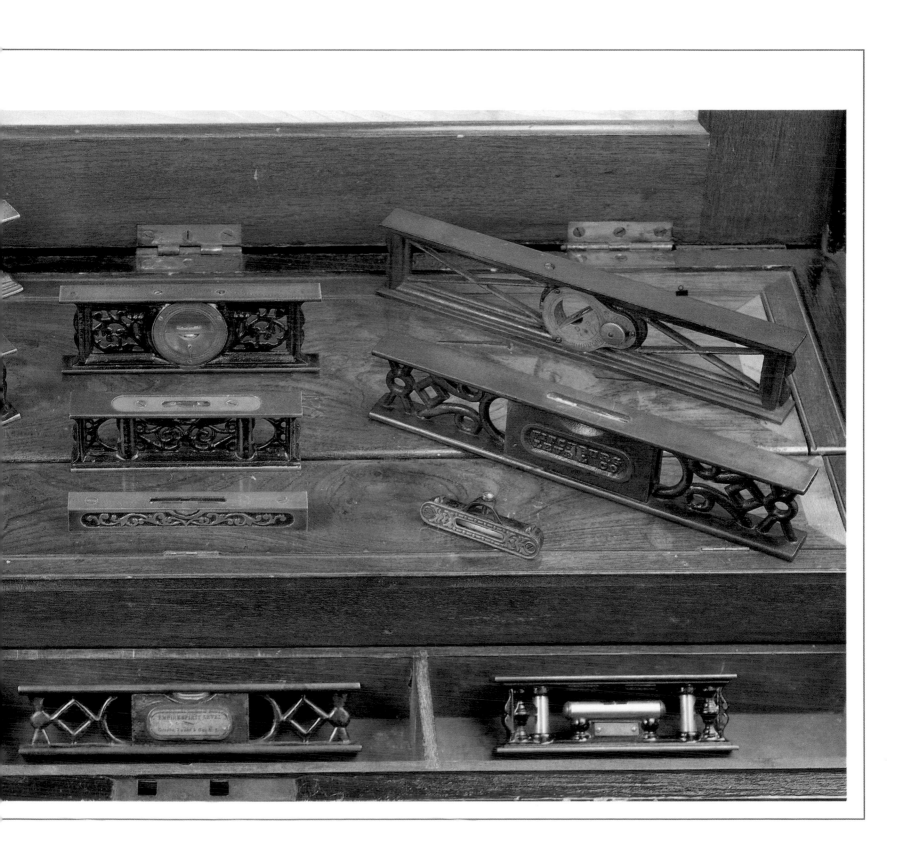

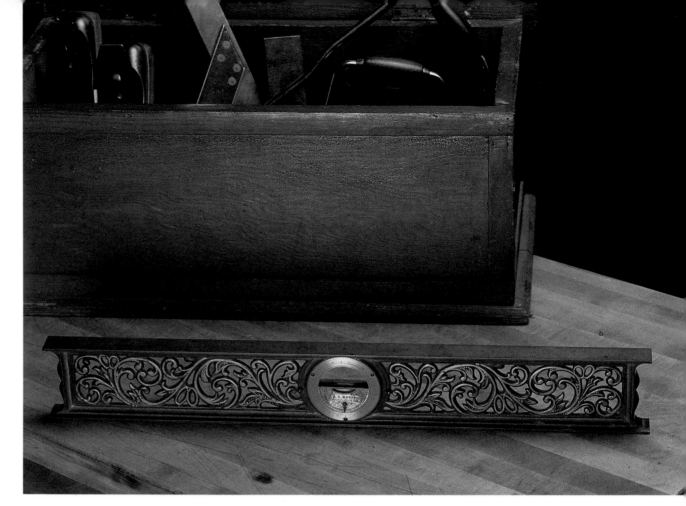

Davis level from Philadelphia Centennial

As its fancy paint job and engraving attest, this cast-iron L. L. Davis Level Co. level was likely to have been created for the Philadelphia Centennial Exposition of 1876. The Davis Co. had a large booth at that event, and this 24-in.-long model was one of the highlights. Although this model of Davis level was manufactured with gold painted decorations, production models lacked the fine detail and fancy brush strokes lavished on this exposition level. Davis used female labor to do the painting. Fancy engraved curlicues surround the company name (detail, right), which was normally just stamped into the inclinometer.

David Kretchun collection

Four cast-iron carpenter's levels

These levels, produced in the heyday of cast-iron tools, are (top to bottom): a spindle-style Davis Patent level; a Davis Patent level made by the M. W. Robinson Co.; a Millers Falls 1884 Goddell's patent, the first model they produced with an adjustable level vial; and an ornate, early-model Davis Level and Tool Co. inclinometer.

From the collection of Don Rosebrook

Large engraved plumb bob

Large and fat, this brass plumb bob was engraved after it was
turned by its maker. To add weight, plumb bobs were often filled
with steel shot, lead, or mercury.

From the collection of Steve Johnson

Brass, steel, and ivory plumb bobs

Like a display of shiny Christmas
ornaments, this bevy of plumb
bobs represents a wide range of
sizes and types available to
woodworkers over the past
150 years or so. While most
plumb bobs were constructed
of brass, there are also a few
examples made from iron or
steel, and one of turned ivory.

From the collection of Steven F. Dice

Plumb bobs, scrimshawed ivory and brass

The two plumb bobs shown above represent both present and past eras. The plumb bob at left was recently made by miniaturist Paul Hamler, though he used an antique ivory billiard cue ball for the turned body. The surface of the bob has a scrimshaw scene (by Dominic Micalizzi) of a sperm whale breaching the water and upending a long boat and its crew. The other side has a nautical vignette of an anchor and harpoons, decoratively surrounded by rope. The antique brass-bodied plumb bob at right is stamped "John Lackman, 1870" with the initials "JEA" below it (probably the owner's stamp). Its sharp steel point is sheathed beneath a protective threaded brass cap, lest the owner impale himself.

From the collection of George Gaspari

Engraved brass plumb bob with wood reel

The fancy engraving on the body suggests that this brass plumb bob was likely to have been a presentation tool, possibly a gift to a retiring carpenter from his colleagues. The steel-pointed bob still has its original line reel, which was lathe turned from boxwood.

From the collection of Steven F. Dice

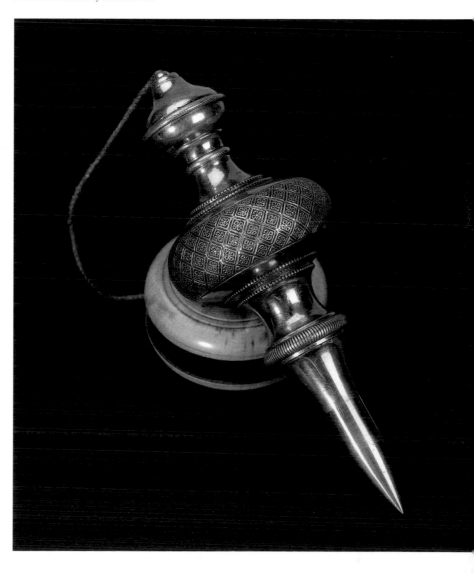

HANDPLANES OF FANCY

Before the advent of powered woodworking machinery, planes were the workhorses of every woodworker's tool chest. These simple hand tools could surface and dress lumber, flatten panels, joint edges, smooth surfaces, cut and trim joinery, shape moldings, contour parts, and much more. Woodworkers in dozens of different professions—coach builders, carpenters, coopers, wheelwrights, coffin makers—all used an extensive selection of planes, scrapers, and spokeshaves to carry out their daily tasks.

Today, most of these trades have vanished, victims of the high-stepping march of modern industry, which has substituted machinery and power tools for hand work and assembly lines for one-of-a-kind craftsmanship. But despite the fact that modern woodworkers have at their disposal all sorts of powered and mechanized equipment for planing, jointing, and smoothing wood, I know of no small-shop cabinetmakers or furniture makers who don't possess at least a basic complement of handplanes.

Before there were handplanes, wood was planed, shaped, and smoothed with more primitive tools, such as adzes and chisels. But even when wielded by skilled hands, chisels and adzes are poor tools for bringing large planks to true flatness or for preparing edges of boards to be accurately joined.

The first tools that could be called handplanes were made by the Romans before the time of Christ. Their basic design was, in essence, a jig for a chisel: The plane maintained the blade at a fixed angle relative to the stock and limited its projection through the sole to regulate depth of cut. Its handles provided a comfortable means for the user to hold the tool and apply force to the cut. The design was enormously successful, so much so that it has remained basically unchanged for more than two millennia! Except for the Middle Ages and the Renaissance, when craftsmen eschewed most planes and instead chose to embellish their wood surfaces with carvings, planes have been in nearly continuous use since Roman times by cabinetmakers, carpenters, and artisans in related trades.

The humble bench plane (in the form of jointer, jack, smooth, or block plane) provided a means of performing ordinary woodworking tasks such as flattening and smoothing with speed and efficiency. From this basic design came literally hundreds of more specialized planes. Each was developed and refined for a specific purpose: to cut rabbets, grooves, chamfers, dadoes, beads, sliding dovetails, or molding profiles. While there are probably thousands of examples of wood-, wood/metal-, and metal-bodied handplanes that have survived from the last few hundred years or so, most of the planes featured in this chapter are metal planes from the second half of the 19th century.

The first part of this chapter presents a small selection of early metal planes from Europe: England, Scotland, France, Austria, and Italy. The next part of the chapter features plow and combination planes, which are among the most spectacular woodworking tools ever made! From the earliest all-wood plow planes made from exotic materials—ebony, rosewood, or even elephant ivory—to the fantastically ornate bronze or extravagantly painted cast-iron plow planes, these tools (see pp. 44-55) are among the greatest treasures to be found in a vintage tool chest. They were physically large, so there was ample room for adornment, such as the elaborate inlays or decorative carvings done by both

users and manufacturers. There also were clever mechanisms for adjusting and locking a plow plane's fence, which sometimes made the tools more visually interesting. Other components, such as turned locking knobs and ivory arm tips, added a further degree of ornament and made fancy plow planes all the more special.

The next section of the chapter covers an assortment of specialty planes, the latter often associated with a particular trade, such as coopering or instrument making. Included are remarkable English and Scottish miter planes, intricate compass planes, and curvaceous coachmaker's planes.

The chapter concludes with a small selection of tools that are first cousins of the handplane: spokeshaves,

beading tools, and scrapers. Like planes, these tools all have an adjustable blade held in a body and a sole. In the days before a craftsman could turn to an electric router to make moldings or round over sharp edges, and when even sheets of sandpaper had to be made by hand, craftsmen depended on these simple tools to shape and smooth their woodwork.

The planes, spokeshaves, and scrapers featured in this chapter are among the rarest and most decorative ever made. But far from being a collection of fantasy implements designed primarily for display, each and every tool shown on these pages was made to be used in the shop. Even the fanciest ones show signs of wear, and were built sturdily enough to survive until now. I trust you will find all the tools interesting and enjoyable, even if they tend to make the "daily user" planes most of us have in our tool chests seen rather ordinary by comparison. ✳

Early Scottish miter planes

Early Scottish metal miter planes have an appearance and construction that's very different from their same-named wooden brethren. The body of this type of plane is a metal box with wooden "infills" front and rear that function as handles and a bed for the blade. The steel or brass sides are joined to the sole with pins or with dovetails (which you can see at the lower edge of the plane in the foreground). Typically, the soles on this type of plane project beyond the front, and sometimes the rear, of the body. The blades are set at a very low angle, and the mouth of the plane is usually very narrow (as small as $\frac{1}{32}$ in.), so these planes are capable of taking very fine cuts in squirrely-grained hardwoods. Both planes shown here have ebony infills. The longer plane has a brass diamond inlay in the front grip; the shorter plane an square ivory inlay.

From the collection of John and Janet Wells

Early bench plane

This metal bench plane, probably of French origin, is thought to be an early example of the use of cast iron (as opposed to forged iron) in handplanes. The unusually shaped front infill, carved from rosewood, works with the upturned portion of the body casting just behind it, forming a rather Spartan front grip. The 9-in.-long plane has a rear handle and wedge carved from walnut.

From the collection of Valdis Petersons

Continental miter planes

Although they might look a bit crude compared to the best fully adjustable metal bench planes available today, these early European miter planes would likely be as serviceable now as they were when new, approximately four centuries ago. Likely to have been made in Italy (left) and Austria (right), both planes have bodies and blades forged from iron and a wooden wedge to hold the plane iron steady, yet allow fine adjustment—a system that has been used on handplanes for hundreds of years.

From the collection of John and Janet Wells

40

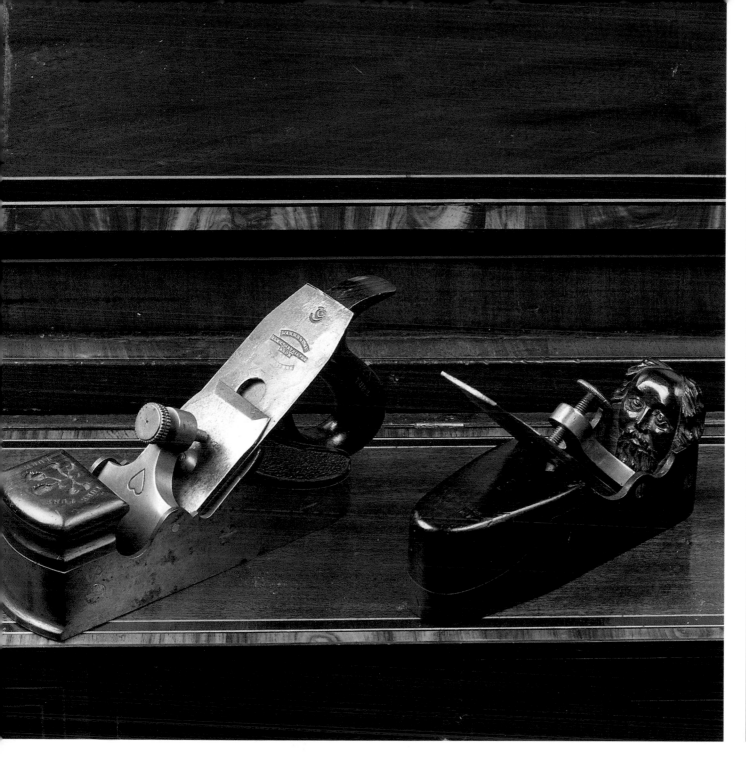

British miter planes

These miter planes are representative of high-quality planes made in the British Isles in the mid-19th century. The plane at left is marked "Alex P. Mathieson & Son" and has a half-moon and star stamped on its iron. The lever cap is stamped with the town, Glasgow, and a heart. A thistle and leaves are carved into the plane's front grip. The plane at right has a cast-iron body with rosewood infill. The front grip is carved in the form of a man's face (which bears a striking resemblance to William Shakespeare). It has a brass lever cap iron stamped "F. G. Pearson & Co., Sheffield."

Collection of Ronald W. Pearson, D.O.

Decorative plane with screwdriver

Probably made by its user, this fancy wood plane has a Mouleon Bros. cast-steel iron and the initials "D. P." stamped into its rosewood and brass body. Its adornments include cast-brass side plates and a lever cap that bears embossed stars and brass ornaments punched with decorative patterns. The plane was worn to the point where its mouth needed to be narrowed to allow a finer cut, so a piece of boxwood in the shape of a minaret dome was inlaid into the sole just ahead of the mouth. Probably the most unusual thing about the plane is that loosening a small brass knob just ahead of the front grip allows removal of a brass-handled screwdriver, seen in the foreground. The screwdriver can be used to adjust the iron.

Collection of Ronald W. Pearson, D.O.

WOOD VS. METAL BODIES

For many centuries, wood was the primary material for the construction of all manner of planes, from tiny violinmaker's shaping planes to cooper's jointer planes (which were so large that they were used inverted on a stand, the workpiece moved over the upturned sole of the plane). Many of the early planes were made by their owners to suit the needs of their trades—cabinetmaking, coffin making, or coach building. There were plenty of manufacturers in Europe and North America that produced wood-bodied bench planes over the centuries. Among the earlier manufacturers of standardized wooden bench planes were the Dutch (see the sidebar on p. 170).

Although developed as early as Roman times, the metal-bodied handplane was abandoned for many centuries, until revived in the early 1800s. After a transitional period, where metal components that provided a blade bed and means of setting and locking the blade were mated with wood bodies, the metal handplane again emerged. Most of the examples that appear in this chapter, and throughout the book, were made between 1825 and 1900, which was a sort of "golden age" for the metal plane. England and America were the countries that dominated the plane industry during this period.

Sandusky centerwheel plow plane

This magnificent ebony and ivory Sandusky centerwheel plow plane has a most interesting recent history. It seems that American toolmaker Bob Baker reproduced this 1880s-style plane from existing examples in other woods. Although Sandusky listed an ebony centerwheel plow plane in its price lists, none had ever been found. Leonard Lee, owner of Lee Valley Tools, bought one of Baker's reproductions and featured a photo of it on the cover of his company's 1984 tool catalog. That exposure led to the discovery of the first known ebony Sandusky, then owned by Victoria, British Columbia, cabinetmaker and author John Rodd. Rodd had restored the plane, replacing one of the ivory tips (and engraving his initials, to add a personal touch). Lee subsequently purchased this rare plane, which now resides at Lee Valley Tools headquarters in Ottawa, Ontario.

Courtesy of Lee Valley Tools

19th-century wood plow planes

The four planes shown here represents some of the more attractive and interesting wood plow planes that were "daily users" in the 19th century. At left, a rosewood plow made by the Greenfield Tool Company in the 1870s and sold under a different brand name. It has boxwood arms with ivory tips. Each of the nuts (which adjust and lock the fence) is made from a ring of rosewood sandwiched between two rings of ivory. At center rear is an E. W. Carpenter boxwood plow made in Lancaster County, Pennsylvania, and patented in 1838. The plane's arms are threaded through the body and are adjusted by turning the rosewood knobs at the ends of the arms. The plane at center front was made in the mid-1800s by John Dennison, a plane maker from Connecticut. This ebony and boxwood plane has two very unusual elongated nuts for locking the fence. The plane at right is a Greenfield Plane Co. No. 522 with an ebony body, a boxwood arm, and large ivory locking nuts.

From the collection of Don Rosebrook

Single-knob plow plane

One of the most unusual planes ever is this single-armed plow, signed T. J. McMaster and made in the 1840s. Turning the ivory "doorknob" at the end of the arm engages a pair of hand-cut gears, rotating a threaded shaft that moves the fence back and forth. The plane's ebony body is adorned with brass hardware and a steel skate.

From the collection of Don Rosebrook

Somewhere around 1870, carpenters and cabinetmakers were first offered an alternative to owning an entire shelf full of wooden molding planes: the metal combination plane. A single plow-type plane with an adjustable fence and depth stop could be fitted with a wide variety of cutters, allowing it to perform tasks such as plowing tongues and grooves and cutting beads and fillets. And in contrast to wood-bodied planes, iron planes weren't vulnerable to warpage, which could hinder or even ruin good performance. Both points made the metal combination plane attractive to the journeyman carpenter, who liked the idea of having only one versatile, road-worthy tool to transport instead of a burdensome boxful.

Because the complexity of most combination planes made them expensive to produce, manufacturers started making them more ornate, introducing models that were made of showy materials or had elaborate decorations and fancy paint jobs. These offered more apparent value for the dollar and made the high prices easier for a craftsman on a modest salary to justify.

Mayo combination plane

This coppery-bronze painted Mayo Patent plane is a later model than the gaily painted plane shown in the top photo on p. 50. The cutters in front of it show only a small number of the possible shapes that combination planes could be used to cut. Each cutter has a lengthwise groove and small steel dowel "handle" to make it easier to fit and remove and adjust. The name "Mayo" is spelled out by script initials, one each on the plane's four brass locking screws (one for the fence, one for the blade, and two for the skate). This lovely plane was produced only for a few years before the company went out of business.

From the collection of Don Rosebrook

Sandusky rosewood plow plane

The Sandusky Plane Company of Sandusky, Ohio, produced an extensive line of handsome wooden plow planes, including its model No. 132, shown on the facing page. While not as fancy as the fanciest plow planes of the period, the beautiful Brazilian rosewood construction, elegant lines, and crisp details—note the rope carving around the perimeter of the locking knobs—make this plane a classic.

David Kretchun collection

Moseley ivory plow plane

Constructed primarily of elephant ivory, this spectacular plow plane by John Moseley and Son is said to have been made for one of the world's first international trade fairs: the famous Crystal Palace Exhibition of 1851 in London. The plane, which has brass fittings and German silver trim, is extensively adorned with scrimshaw, including the program cover design for the Exhibition and French and English flags. Notice that the plane's ivory arms have silver caps only on one end and get set for a shock: After the Moseley firm was sold in 1892, someone sawed about 2 in. off the ends of the arms so the plane would fit into a display case!

Courtesy of Lee Valley Tools

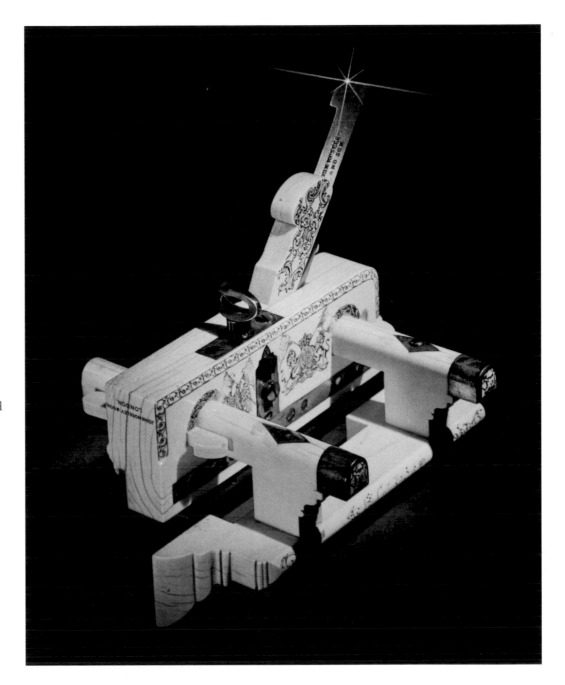

Phillips improved plow plane, Mayo patent

This decorative Phillips plow plane from 1872 was the "improved" version of a series of boxy-looking planes the company produced earlier. Designed by Matthias Mayo, the gaily painted plane bears his name and patent date in the rectangular recess at the front edge of the fence extension. It is speculated that Mayo's streamlined design may have been influenced by the showy Miller's Patent planes of the time (see the photo on the facing page). The slotted boss atop the fence was a useful feature; it allowed locking of the fence on the extension rod without the locking screw coming in direct contact with the rod—and marring it over repeated tightenings.

Courtesy of Jon Zimmers

Plow plane with star inlays

A most decorative and unusual plow plane made by A. McBride, of Louisville, Kentucky, c. 1845. The rosewood-bodied plane's silver and brass inlays are as they were when the plane was originally manufactured.

From the collection of Don Rosebrook

Although small manufacturers patented scores of different designs for metal combination planes in the late 19th century, few patents were to prove as significant as Charles G. Miller's "Miller's Patent" planes. His idea underwent many design changes, from a basic plow plane to a plow with a removable filister bed to a complex combination plane with a multitude of cutters. Most planes based on Miller's design were manufactured by the Stanley Rule & Level Company, which bought Miller's patent in 1870.

Stanley produced thousands of regular Miller's Patent planes from the late 1800s to the mid-1940s, as well as a few models that were made in limited numbers and are rare today. These include the No. 50 (see p. 55). But there is none rarer than the plane shown in the photo at right, thought to be Charles G. Miller's own original patent model. This bronze plane is virtually identical to its patent drawing (Patent No. 104,753), which is dated June 28, 1870—yet the plane was never manufactured in this exact form. This is the full-size, working model, which at nearly 10 in. long, is fancier than many of the subsequent production models.

This is considered to be Charles G. Miller's own original patent model for the famous Miller's Patent plane series manufactured by Stanley. With its ebony handle with ivory inlays and its little ivory finials atop the plane's six adjustment knobs, this bronze prototype is considerably different from the subsequent production models.

From the collection of Bud Steere

Phillips bronze plow plane, detail

This detail of the engraving on the bronze
Phillip's "plough" plane (facing page) clearly
shows the makers name and trademark.
The small knob at the front (right) locks
the plane's depth stop.

Collection of Eric M. Peterson

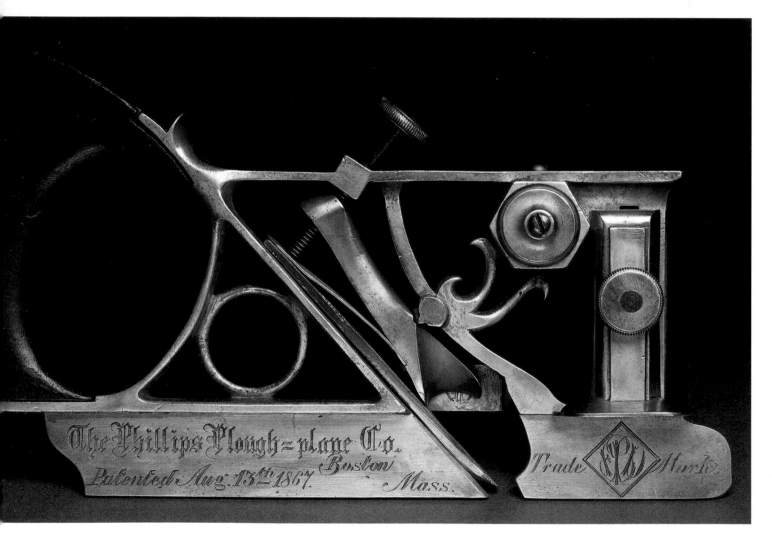

Phillips bronze plow plane

Can you believe anyone would throw out a tool that was this beautiful? Yet this plane was found by a lucky scavenger at a New Hampshire dump in 1982! This bronze-bodied, rosewood-handled Phillips "plough" plane is not only attractive, it's rare. It was likely made as a special presentation piece, and only two are known to exist. The plane's bronze body and fence were cast by the Metallic Compression Casting Company, of Boston, Massachusetts. Most metal plow planes of this era are dual armed, but for simplicity and possibly weight savings Boston carpenter Russell Phillips designed his planes to have a single, heavy arm supporting the fence. A groove that runs the length of the top of the arm engages the locking screw, thereby keeping the fence aligned with the plane's skate.

Collection of Eric M. Peterson

Miller's Patent plow-plane pair, iron and gunmetal

Among the most popular metal combination planes of their time, the famous Stanley "Miller's Patent" planes were available as the cast-iron-bodied No. 43 (left) or the gunmetal-bronze-bodied No. 42 (right), complete with a cast-iron filletster bed. Despite their decorative looks, these planes were real workhorses, capable of plowing grooves and rabbets, cutting tongue-and-groove joints, and more.

Courtesy of Jon Zimmers

Miller's Patent No. 50 bronze plow plane

One of the fanciest woodworking tools ever manufactured, the Miller's Patent No. 50 plow plane is true artistry in bronze. The snakeskin-like chasing that covers much of the plane not only sets off the intricate Victorian scrollwork, but also adds to the serpentine lines of this rare plane. A single rosewood knob on the end of the front extension rod helps the user keep the fence against the stock for a straight cut. Even the knurled fence-locking knobs have been located on the underside of the casting so as not to interfere with the operator—or the graceful lines of the tool. A small knurled knob atop the cutter adjusts the depth of cut.

From the collection of John and Janet Wells

English shoulder and miter planes

Both of these English metal planes have remarkably sculptural forms. The 8-in.-long shoulder plane in the background has a solid gunmetal body with ebonized and light wood infills and a wedge. The bronze gunmetal adds an aesthetic touch as well as heft—a good thing when doing sensitive work, such as truing up the shoulders of a tenon. The 6-in.-long miter plane in the foreground also appears to be cast bronze, but in fact has a cast-iron body with an unusual applied brass covering, which is probably purely decorative. The infill and wedge are carved with a series of flutes that resembles the body of a scarab beetle.

From the collection of Roger B. Phillips

English and Scottish planes

Here's a set of English and Scottish planes, representing the work of some of the finest plane makers in the late 19th century. At right is an English smooth plane made by Ibbotson & Company, with a heavy bronze body, a gracefully sculpted lever cap, and rosewood infills. The unusual-looking plane at left is a bronze-bodied Lancashire pattern shoulder plane, supplied by T. J. Gardner, of Bristol, England. This plane can be used for trimming either the base or side of a rabbet. In the middle of the photo are three block planes. At center right is a No. 32 block plane by Norris & Son of London (1860-1940) with a cast-iron body and sole and a rosewood wedge and infill. In the middle is a Stewart Spiers plane (1840-1920) made in Ayr, Scotland. This 5-in.-long plane has a cast-iron body and bronze lever cap. The bronze-bodied Norris No. 31 (at center left) has a brass lever cap in lieu of the older-style wooden wedge.

From the collection of Steve Johnson

While coachmakers made use of many of the standard woodworking planes found in the toolboxes of carpenters and cabinetmakers, they also had dozens of edge tools specially adapted to their needs. Most of these are small-sized planes, with short soles designed to work the curved panels and frames found in the wooden horse-drawn coaches of yore. The compact planes are also handy when working in confined spaces, such as inside a partially assembled coach.

The cast-iron plane shown in the photo at left, from the collection of John and Janet Wells, is a T-rabbet-style plane (as are the bronze coachmaker's planes shown below). This style of plane has a sole that is wider than the handle (or, on a wooden plane, the stock). This type of design allows more room for the craftsman's hands when working in a tight spot, such as an inside corner. The plane at left also has a convex sole designed for trimming around gentle hollow curves or compound-curved surfaces.

These coachmaker's T-rabbet planes, with their fluid body lines, are somewhat reminiscent of the sort of work they were made to create: the curvaceous bodies of the horse-drawn coaches and carriages of the day. Both of the bronze-bodied planes shown at right were user made from heavy alloys that lend the planes weight and stability during tricky cutting.

From the collection of Steven F. Dice

Bailey Victor compass plane No. 20

Known as the Victor No. 20 Adjustable Circular plane, this compass plane was patented by Leonard Bailey and produced sometime after 1875. It uses a single screw to flex the front and back ends of the sole at the same time, resulting in an even curve (earlier compass planes required users to adjust the sole front and back separately). Once the 12½-in. long sole is set for a convex or concave cut, the adjuster is locked by a knurled ring. The decorative front and back knobs (detail, p. 182) serve as handles.

Mel Miller Collection

Bailey No. 1½ with nickel trim

As on many other block planes, the blade on the Bailey No. 1½ is set at a low angle to the sole. This makes the plane terrific for cleanly trimming hardwood end grain. The nickel-plated front knob loosens to allow the mouth of the plane to be adjusted, much as it does in many modern block planes. The rear handle acts as a grip or can be pushed with the palm for more forceful planing. It can be detached to make the plane shorter when working in a confined area, such as inside a box or drawer.

From the collection of John and Janet Wells

Burlington's Patent Clapboard plane

Burlington's Patent Clapboard plane, made from gunmetal and patented in 1874, combined a basic block plane with a square and a marking gauge. Hence, one tool could be used to lay out and true up the edges and ends of clapboards, saving the carpenter from having to carry and use several tools. The tool was developed for the manufacturer by Burkner F. Burlington, who was probably the carpenter who designed the tool, and Joseph Cartwright, a Massachusetts hardware-store owner who likely thought Burlington's idea had enough merit to bankroll the manufacture of the tool.

From the collection of Clifford R. Sapienza

Lee bronze chamfer plane

With its filigree painted handle and gunmetal frame and fence, this Lee's Patent Stop Chamfer plane, from the Edward Jacobs collection, was the fancy version of the company's basic black japanned iron chamfer plane, commonly seen in late-19th-century cabinet shops. Made c. 1885 by Horace Thurston in Providence, Rhode Island, the plane originally came with 11 different cutters, allowing it to do a lot more than just putting a simple chamfer on the edge of a panel.

Courtesy Roger K. Smith, Patented Transitional & Metallic Planes In America, 1827-1927; *(photo by Joseph Szaszfai)*

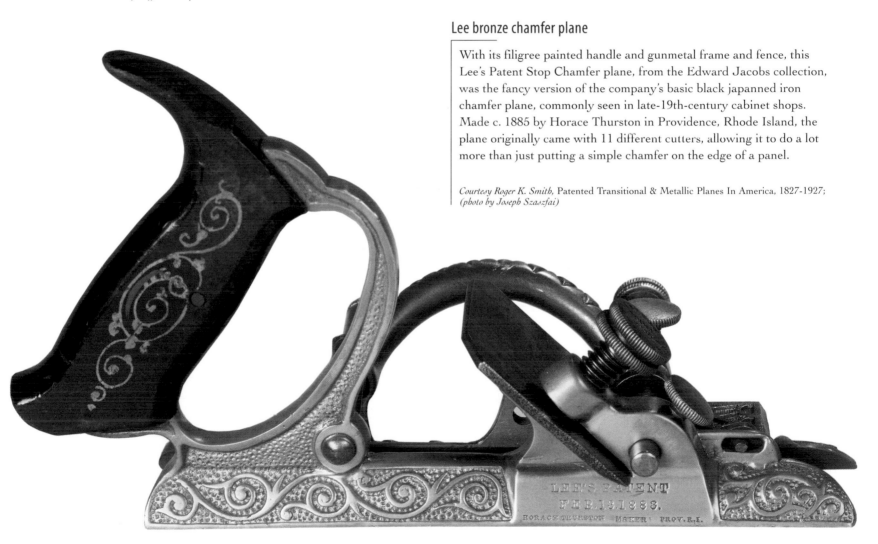

Toolbox set of planes

This matching set of planes was created for a customer (likely a journeyman carpenter or cabinetmaker), along with the beautiful custom case that houses them. The case, built from bird's-eye maple, walnut, and cherry, is reinforced with sturdy brass straps and decorative hardware. The five planes—a razee smoother, two jacks, a fore, and a jointer— have bodies, handles, and wedges made from maple. Each plane has a small brass diamond inlaid into the top of the wedge and a stylish rosette on the top of the front end of the body. These serve as striking points for setting and removing the iron.

From the collection of Patrick and Lisa Leach

Morris' Patent smooth plane

This Morris' Patent smooth plane has an iron body with applewood infill, handles, and a wedge, all of which have an understated pattern of wheat carved into the surface with a fine V-gouge. The sole of the 11½-in.-long plane has a diamond pattern originally intended to help reduce friction (see the sidebar on p. 145).

From the collection of Clifford R. Sapienza

Preston spokeshaves

At a time when most English toolmakers were located in Sheffield, Edward Preston and Sons made very fine-quality planes and spokeshaves in Birmingham. Three of the more ornate models are shown here. With bodies made of nickel-plated cast iron, these spokeshaves represent the complete range of sizes the company made: from the 10-in.-long No. 1391 (which used a 2⅛-in.-wide cutter), to the 7-in.-long No. 1374, down to the 6-in.-long No. 1373.

From the collection of Patrick and Lisa Leach

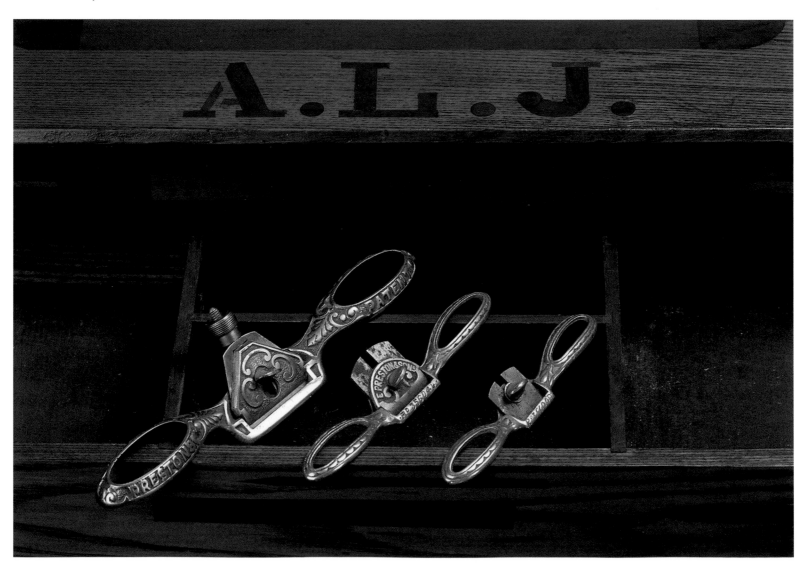

Windsor beaders

The three tools at left are Windsor Beaders, so called because they were patented in Windsor, Vermont (in 1885, by Lawrence Poole and Orlando Williams). The older model (called the first type), shown at front, has a one-piece handle, body, and sole made of cherry. The other two beaders (called the second type) have hardwood bodies and a brass or steel plate and fence supporting the cutter head. On both types, the cutter head has several different beading patterns; the head rotates to allow pattern selection.

From the collection of Steven F. Dice

Bailey Patent scraper

The Bailey Patent scraper plane's cast-bronze body and turned rosewood handles make it the Mercedes of all scraper planes, but its design was the basis for the Volkswagen of the genre: the Stanley No. 12, which was produced in great numbers until 1957. The blade-adjustment mechanism, based on the first patent granted to inventor and toolmaker Leonard Bailey, allows the cutter to be tilted in relation to the sole, thereby providing an easy and accurate means of adjusting the depth of cut.

From the collection of John and Janet Wells

Fox box scraper

Basic tools used for everything from scraping the labels off shipping crates to taking the coarse tool marks from a surface to be smoothed, box scrapers were an important item in every cabinetmaker's toolbox. The tool shown here has a simple wood body to which a scraper blade and lever cap are mounted. A bright paint job and attractive decal promote the maker—Fox Manufacturing, of Milwaukee Wisconsin—and also make an otherwise ordinary tool a little more festive.

From the collection of Patrick and Lisa Leach

French long-handled scrapers

Bearing only the name of their maker, Louis Cenzinec, these long-handled tools are a pair of early French scrapers. The 14- in.-long cocobolo handles connect to cast-bronze frames with rosewood infills. A wedge secures the scraper blade in each. The tools were likely used for smoothing wooden floors prior to finishing.

From the collection of Don Rosebrook

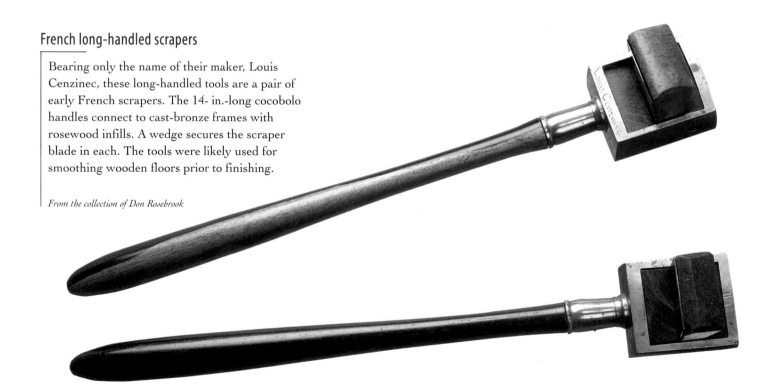

Boufford's Patent scraper

This cast-iron tool, patented by its creator, Joseph Boufford, in 1899, has a 12¾-in.-long handle that holds a 2¾-in.-wide blade, giving the user considerable leverage. The decorative floral motif cast into the handle is unique for a tool of this kind.

From the collection of the Michael Armstrong Family

TOOLS FOR HAMMERING AND DRILLING

Driving nails and boring holes are basic tasks necessary for a very wide range of woodworking undertakings, from building a barn to assembling a cabinet to trimming out a boat. Nary a woodworker exists who doesn't have at least one hammer and one drill or brace in his or her tool kit. But the contemporary forms of these tools that we are familiar with don't reveal much about the fascinating and sometimes decorative forms these tools have taken in the past.

The hammer is one of the most ancient implements in the human tool kit, and also one of the most versatile: It was used for obtaining food, performing ceremonies, and building shelter, as well as for making other tools. Hammers have been used in a vast number of different trades to drive fasteners and stakes, shape metal and stone, split wood, tenderize meat, and even knock snow and ice off horses' hooves. Because a hammer can be used to fashion other metal tools, it is sometimes referred to as the "king of tools."

The hammer has evolved through many forms and constructions, from a stone attached to the end of a stick to a modern forged-steel tool. A staple of the carpenter's chest, the modern claw hammer has remained roughly the same basic shape since ancient times.

The earliest hammers with forged heads were made by the Egyptians as early as 6000 B.C. This isn't to say that the tool hasn't changed over the course of time: The shape of the head and the means of its attachment to the handle have gone through countless variations (see the sidebar on p. 71).

Even among the tools that we can call woodworking hammers, there's a lot of variety. In Victorian times, there were ornate "household" hammers that were designed to handle a variety of domestic chores, such as driving a nail to hang auntie's portrait or knocking back the upholstery tacks that got pulled out when kitty attacked the fabric on the underside of the divan. For the more serious work of the cabinetmaker, clawless hammers (in the style of what we contemporarily know as the Warrington hammer) with both flat and tapered heads are marvelous for driving a row of brads to attach a strip of molding or for setting the escutcheon pins that mount a piece of brass hardware. And no carpenter's belt would be complete without a sturdy claw hammer with a head massive enough to drive the big nails it takes to build walls or remodel a parlor or a porch.

The claws on carpenter's hammers are a topic of discussion all by themselves. Over the decades, various claw designs have sought to improve the grab of the claw on the shank of a bent nail or allow a nail to be started single-handed. Some oddball multi-claw creations were meant to give the user more leverage when pulling nails (see the sidebar on p. 77).

No less important to the woodworker is a bit brace or drill with which to bore holes. Although not as old as the hammer (the oldest brace known to exist was recovered from the ship's carpenter's kit on the *Mary Rose*, an English flagship that sank in the year 1545), these boring tools have taken just a few basic forms over several hundred years. The earliest wood drill was probably no more than a sharpened stick or straight bone rotated between the hands of a thick-browed proto-craftsman, perhaps to fashion a tool or to shape a chunk of wood into a piece of sculpture.

Drill designs that are only slightly more sophisticated have survived into recent centuries. The bow drill, the principal form of which was likely used to generate the friction and heat necessary to start a fire, was commonly used by 19th-century jewelers and cabinetmakers, the latter for drilling small holes for mounting hardware or starting screws. This drill uses a bow-and-arrow-like bow with a string wrapped around a drum-like portion of the tool's body to spin a bit back and forth. Somewhat similar in principle, the Archimedean drill has a twisted shank and threaded knob that the user moves up and down to spin the bit.

The back-and-forth action of a bow drill or many Archimedean drills worked fine for small bits and holes but not for boring clean holes in large sizes. For that came the innovation of the bit brace, which rotates a bit continuously in a single direction. The bit, of course, was designed to cut while spinning in one direction (typically clockwise), but it removed stock more quickly and cleanly than spade-point bi-directional bits, and, with the development of twist-shanked bits, ejected chips better as well.

While the basic shape of the brace has changed little, the innovations in the design of brace handles and the means for holding a bit are staggering (the number of patents for brace chucks alone could fill a volume!). Similarly, designs for braces and drills abound, including folding braces, braces that let you drill into tight corners and at an angle, and gear-driven drills (some of which allow you to change the speed of bit rotation). Many geared drills are not only visually interesting, but also showcase the mechanical ingenuity of their designers.

This chapter will present photographs of some of the finest hammers, drills, and braces ever to occupy a carpenter's or woodworker's tool kit, including contemporary tools as well as vintage examples. Whether wrought one at a time by a solitary blacksmith working in a tiny country shop or designed and manufactured in the tens of thousands by a huge international tool corporation, each of the implements featured here has an inspiring character all its own. ✖

Keeping the head on a hammer from flying off its handle used to be one heck of a problem. Basic iron hammer heads used to be forged from a small billet of iron that was hammered into shape. A hole punched through the billet served as a mounting for the end of the wood handle, which was wedged in place. However, given the forces generated when driving a nail, the small contact between the handle and head led to easy detachment.

To cure this problem, blacksmiths and toolmakers came up with different strategies for making a more secure connection between the head and handle. One common design was the strap-head hammer, in which long forged-iron straps extended down from the head and were riveted to the handle (see the photo at left). The strap-head hammers shown in the photo are from the collection of Dan Comerford. They were made by the same blacksmith, though his name is lost to us today.

The most significant improvement to the hammer head came from Norwich, New York, toolmaker David Maydole in about 1840. His innovation was a single-piece forged head with an integral flange that extended below the head, creating a much larger socket for a more secure head-handle connection. The "adze-eye" hammer became so popular that Maydole had to go into hammer making full time. He never patented his design, though practically all hammers made since 1900 incorporate his adze-eye head.

Roman hammers

Among the oldest metal-headed hammers ever made were those forged and used by Roman craftsmen. Even before the birth of Christ, they had designed a basic forged-iron head, a classic shape that has changed little in the past 2,000 years. These three ancient hammers were unearthed during archaeological digs in Dorset and Cumbria, England, which the Romans invaded in 55 B.C. Of course, two of the hammers have been fitted with new handles more recently.

From the collection of Dan Comerford

Small wraparound-claw hammers

Manufactured with a total of six different-size heads, there was a Solomon Anderson claw hammer for nearly every nail-driving task, from frame carpentry to installing delicate trim. The two shown here are the smallest sizes Anderson made, with 6-oz. and 8-oz. iron heads.

From the collection of Dan Comerford

Solomon Anderson Patent hammers

The first hammer ever to be patented (in 1845), the Solomon Anderson Patent wraparound-claw hammer had a pair of nail-extracting claws that curved back and rejoined to wrap around the handle. This design gives the claws greater strength and reduces the possibility of breakage during nail removal. Two variations of the hammer are shown here: The hammer in front has a round striking head, while the hammer leaning against the box has a hexagonal head.

From the collection of Bud Steere

Fish-head hammer

Little is known of the origin of this fish-head hammer, other than the fact that two of them are known to exist, indicating that it was manufactured rather than a user-made tool. The hammer's head is cast iron, with a rather small striking face.

Courtesy of Martin J. Donnelly Antique Tools, Bath, N. Y.

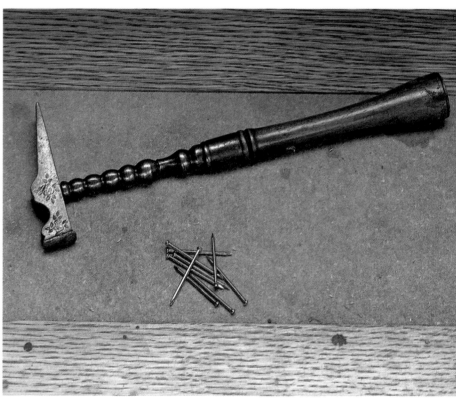

Decorative hammer

This early French hammer has an iron stem and a 3-in.-long head with a wedge-shaped end that allows the user to start small brads and escutcheon pins while holding them between the fingers. Both sides of the head are decorated with a chased pattern of roses and leaves.

From the collection of Roger B. Phillips

Tack-pulling hammer

This hammer, for driving and pulling tacks, was patented by George Capewell in 1896. It has an ornamented cast-iron head with built-in pincers designed to grasp the small head of a tack or brad and hold it firmly for extraction.

From the collection of Steve Johnson

Ornamental hammer

Patented by Charles Hennig in 1901, this small hammer (sometimes called a candy hammer) was made of shiny nickel-plated steel. Designed for small jobs around the house, it was lavishly embellished with Victorian ornament.

From the collection of Don Rosebrook

Goat-head household hammer

It's hard to imagine that toolmaker Mittendorfer Straus ever intended his goat-headed hammer to do any real work, though a cylindrical object in the goat's mouth (possibly a tin can?) makes a usable striking head and its horns form a pair of nail-pulling claws. Patented in 1928, the small bronze-head hammer (which came in two sizes) was more likely used around the house to knock in the occasional tack, smash nut shells, or amuse children.

From the collection of Bud Steere

S earching for a better way to extract a nail, hammer makers had no shortage of ideas for improving on the single-claw design that's de rigueur for nearly all modern carpentry hammers. "If one claw is good, two are better," these inventive makers must have reasoned. Hence, the Unicast hammer, far left, has a small second claw at the base of its adze-eye socket, and the 1902-patented George Voight double-claw hammer, at rear right, has a second full-size claw beneath the first. At center, the BMC jack hammer, which was patented by John Jarrett in 1941, added a rack with notched teeth between a single claw and the handle socket. All three of these designs aimed to give the user a higher point of leverage when extracting long bent nails. However, if two claws are company, three is a crowd: On the hammer at front right, whose maker is unknown, three separate claws are cramped together in such as way that nails of any length are hard to grab and extract. All four hammers are from the collection of Dan Comerford.

Archimedean drills

An Archimedean drill consists of a top handle connected to a threaded shaft that has a slow spiral twist. At the bottom of this shaft is a chuck or socket designed to hold the bit. A handle used to drive the drill (known as the traveling handle) has a nut threaded to engage the spiral thread of the shaft. The bit is rotated for drilling by moving the traveling handle up and down. On many of these tools, the handle motion spins alternately in both directions, so bits were typically V shaped and sharpened on both sides. Archimedean drills were often used for boring small holes in wood or metal, and were handy in cramped quarters, where regular braces were too bulky. Two types of Archimedean drills are shown here. The one at left is the centrifugal type, with a small dumbbell-like metal bar fitted to the shaft near the chuck that acts as a flywheel to keep the drill spinning. An internal ratchet mechanism in the traveling handle allows the shaft to be driven only on the down stroke. The one at right is known as a side-handle or Persian drill. This type of drill was used for delicate tasks, such as jewelry making and even dentistry.

From the collection of Clifford R. Sapienza

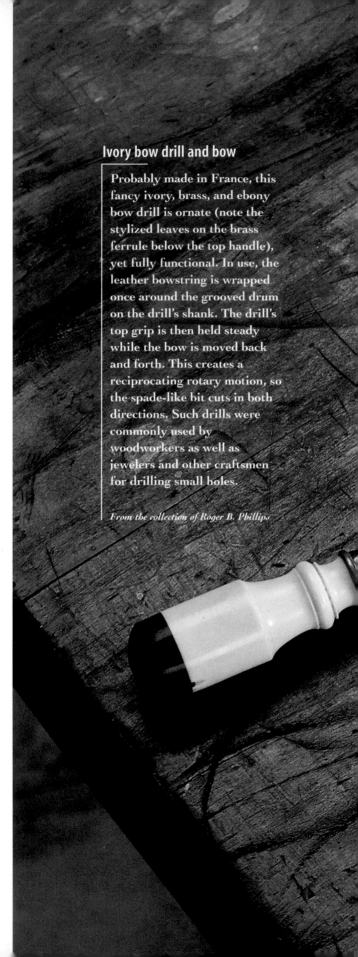

Ivory bow drill and bow

Probably made in France, this fancy ivory, brass, and ebony bow drill is ornate (note the stylized leaves on the brass ferrule below the top handle), yet fully functional. In use, the leather bowstring is wrapped once around the grooved drum on the drill's shank. The drill's top grip is then held steady while the bow is moved back and forth. This creates a reciprocating rotary motion, so the spade-like bit cuts in both directions. Such drills were commonly used by woodworkers as well as jewelers and other craftsmen for drilling small holes.

From the collection of Roger B. Phillips

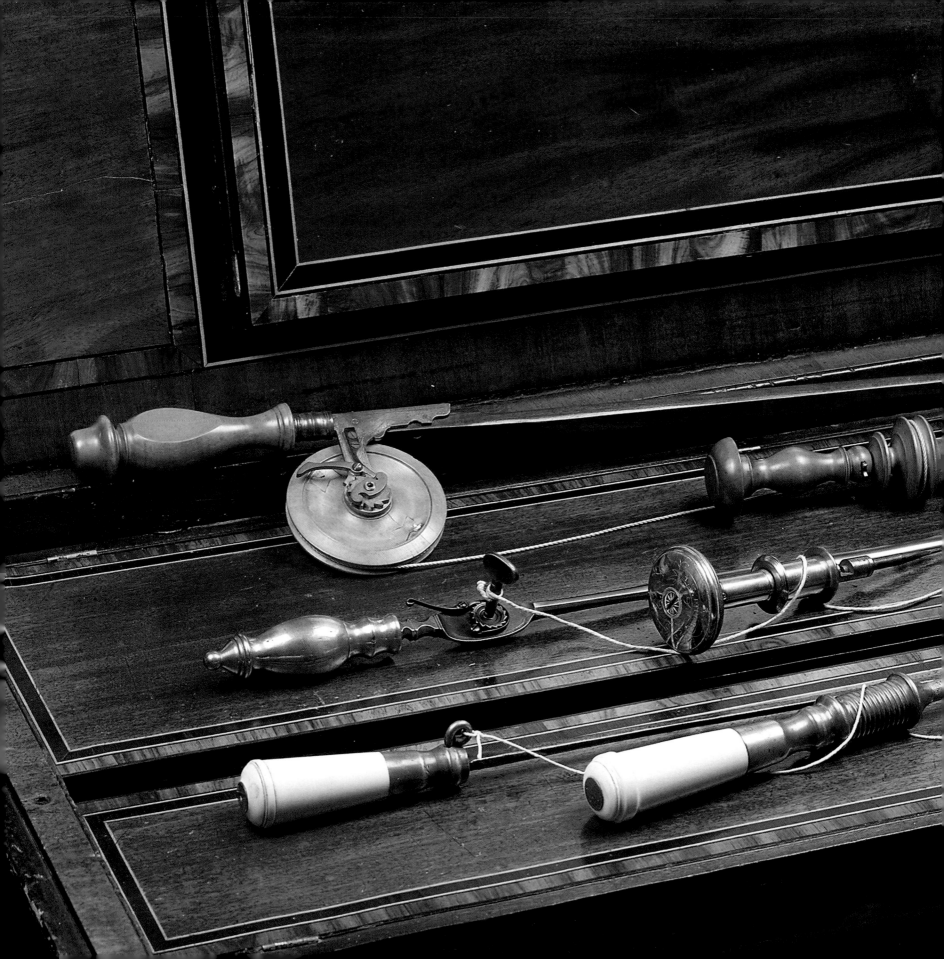

19th-century bow drills

The bow drills shown here represent the most common
designs used by 19th-century woodworkers. At the rear is
a reel-type drill with a pernambuco bow shaped like a
violin bow. The reel and handle are made of boxwood,
with the reel portion constructed in two halves that are
dovetailed together (to thwart warpage, no doubt).
A ratchet mechanism in the bow helps tension the string.
The middle drill is made from brass and steel. The bow
has a well-made ratchet mechanism that allows the
bowstring to be tightened easily. The brass head of the
drill portion bears decorative engraving of the owner's
name surrounded by vines and foliage (detail, below).
The drill and matching bow in the foreground are from
Europe and were probably made c. 1850. The well-made
pair features ivory handles and turned brass fittings.

Collection of Ronald W. Pearson, D.O.

Dolphin brace

This brace is thought to be of French or Italian origin from the mid-1600s. The ornamental iron work is based on a popular stylized dolphin motif often seen in decorative iron work from that period. Housed in a walnut presentation case made by its owner, the brace has turned rosewood handles that replace the original wood handles, which were badly decomposed by the late 1900s. The brace's simple chuck has a tapered, square socket—too small for contemporary bits, but surprisingly similar to more modern European and American designs.

Collection of Ronald W. Pearson, D.O.

Tag-sale treasure

The current owner found this tool, one of the oldest braces in his collection, at a garage sale for only $12 (out of courtesy, he paid the seller $120 for it). Made of oak, the brace is similar in construction to many of the all-wood braces used in the past.

Collection of Eric M. Peterson

Set of Flemish bitstocks

With a size for every occasion, this is a
graduated set of seven Flemish bitstocks,
known as *spykeboors*. The two middle-sized
tools evidently got the most use, but even
the smallest shows signs of considerable
wear. The ferrules on these elm braces are
made of horn or bone, while the heads
are made of boxwood. The arms are carved
with nice details.

Collection of Eric M. Peterson

Fine fakery

Savvy collectors say one must always examine a tool of questionable pedigree with a mind for the characteristics that a tool of that age and type would normally have: Style, materials, wear, patina, and finish must all be considered. At first glance, these unusual braces may seem to be 19th century or even older. However, closer inspection offers lessons in the art of vintage tool fakery. The tiger maple and whalebone bitstock at far left is finely crafted, but shows no wear between rotating components (such as under the head). Also, the type of bit is out of keeping with the dating engraved on the tool (1811). The other brace is made from a section of antler with a burl walnut top handle bearing a whalebone insert. The brace shows no wear—not a surprise, since its grip and chuck are out of line, rendering it totally unusable. Finally, the modern stain and glue help identify this brace as ersatz.

Collection of Eric M. Peterson

Surgeon's braces

Originally designed for boring holes in skulls, early surgeon's braces have been appropriated for use by woodworkers, jewelers, and other craftsmen. All four of the braces shown are French. The one at far left is from the 19th century, while the other three arc most likely much older—similar braces are illustrated in a book from the early 16th century.

Collection of Eric M. Peterson

Five braces: a historical survey

This collection of five braces shows the phases that brace design went through as the tool went from mostly wood to mostly metal. From left to right: a beechwood brace with a very early cast-iron chuck bearing an owner's mark (a small circle with eight star points); a No. 12 Sheffield brace by Henry Parker and Francis Thompson, patented in 1855, featuring an ebony pummel and beechwood body reinforced with brass quarter plates; a rare and decorative brace with flared ends and quarter plates that are inlaid into the Macassar ebony arms; a C & T Pilkington brace, made in Sheffield with its quarter plates surface-mounted on the wood arms (a stronger and easier-to-make design); and finally, the classic brass and wood Ultimatum brace, featuring a metal frame with ebony infills. This example was made by John Morrison, but similar braces were made by a multitude of manufacturers for many years.

Collection of Eric M. Peterson

Brace with coin medallions

Made by Sims of Sheffield, this brass metallic brace has its ebony infills secured with decorative screw heads that have been struck to resemble small coin medallions. Embossed letters on the medallions read "warranted superior."

Collection of Eric M. Peterson

Ivory presentation brace in box

Just as for fancy pistols or fine scientific instruments, presentation cases were used for special woodworking tools, such as this sterling-silver-framed metallic brace with ivory infills. The brace was a gift, presented in 1877 to T. Moore, "upon the occasion of his retirement by his colleagues at Wm. Garrard, Birmingham," as witnessed by a small brass plaque atop the silk-lined box. Known as a "trade brace," this tool, based on the popular Ultimatum pattern, was probably made by William Marples.

Collection of Eric M. Peterson

Very early wood braces held their crudely forged bits in place with friction. Most often, forged drill bits were permanently mounted in a wood bit holder, called a pad. These pads were individually made and fitted to each brace, and were not usually interchangeable between braces. Typically, the pad was secured by a friction fit (a leather shim might be used as well); some brace makers incorporated a wooden thumbscrew or had large-diameter wood threads on the wood pad so that it screwed into place.

Early metal braces had sockets forged into them for flat or square tapered-tang bits that were held in place by friction. Over the decades, dozens of mechanisms were invented and patented for keeping a tapered-tang bit in its socket. In many designs, the bit was held by a notch filed in its tang and locked in place by a catch mechanism. A good example is the brace shown in the photo at right. Made by Benjamin of Avoca, New York, and patented in 1857, the brace, from the collection of Ronald W. Pearson, D.O., has a spring-loaded mech-

anism with a lever that releases the bit (a nice detail is the star chasework around the screws that secure the brass quarter plates). Unfortunately, there were no common chuck systems, and bits couldn't be used with different designs without their notches being refiled.

A significant improvement came with the Universal chuck, first patented by Nelson Spofford in 1859. It held a square-

tang bit in a split square socket forged into the end of the brace. A locking screw drew the two halves of the socket together, so that any tanged bit could be held tightly regardless of its size or notches. Eventually, the even more versatile three-jawed chuck was developed, which could hold both tanged bits and round-shank cutters. It's found on practically all braces and drills today—even electric ones.

Pilkington and Booth Mills braces

The tool at left is a maple brace made by Pilkington in Sheffield, England. It has brass-plated quarter plates and an ebony top grip. The brace at right was made from ebony with German silver quarter plates and an ivory top knob by Booth Mills & Co. of Philadelphia. This special brace was probably made for the 1876 Philadelphia Centennial Exhibition. A similar one may be seen in the E. Mills display at the Smithsonian Institution.

Collection of Ronald W. Pearson, D.O.

89

Jinkinson eagle brace

The magnificent brace on the facing page has cast-bronze quarter plates bearing decorative scrollwork and eagles with outstretched wings (detail, left). Each of the walnut brace's reinforcing quarter plates is a separate casting, and each bears the name of the maker (A. & W. Jinkinson; Cadochan Works) and place of origin (Eldon St., Sheffield, England). A large brass thumbscrew locks the square-tanged bit in place.

Collection of Ronald W. Pearson, D.O.

Whitney eggbeater drill

The decorative eggbeater-style drill shown below on the drawer of a tool chest is a Whitney's No. 10 geared hand drill. Selling originally for $10 per dozen, Whitney drills were sold by Tower and Lyon, a New York City tool seller whose catalogs featured extensive lines of woodworking tools, other trade tools, and even police equipment.

Collection of Roger K. Smith

Bronze and nickel-plated geared drills

These geared drills were both designed for heavy-duty work. The drill at right (which bears no maker's name) has an unusual circular cast-bronze body and an S-shaped crank handle. The large, flat top knob allows a user to apply downward pressure with the chest. The slightly more contemporary brace at far right was made by D. T. Shattuck. The drill's heavy steel frame is nickel plated (to prevent corrosion), and it is fitted with a rosewood knob and crank handle. It features a special quick-locking chuck mechanism.

Collection of Eric M. Peterson

Johnson's Patent drill/drivers

Patented in 1837, these Johnson's Patent push drills are shown here in brass-plated and nickel finishes with their original steel boxes (note the original instruction booklet and the slightly different pattern on each box). With either tool, pushing down on the handle spins the chuck — which may be fitted with a small drill or a screwdriver bit. The tangs of the bits used in Johnson push drills are shaped like a cross, so they lock into the chuck quickly but won't slip.

From the collection of Don Rosebrook

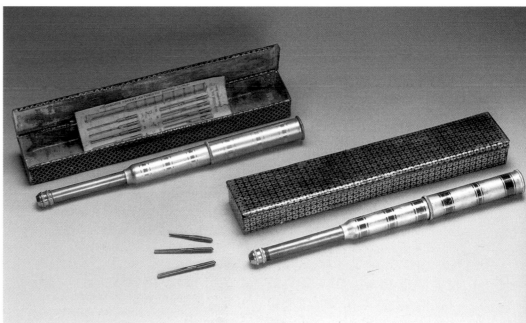

TOOLS FOR SAWING AND SLICING

When you want a simple way to reduce a tree, log, or plank to dimensioned lumber, the ax, handsaw, adze, and chisel are the tools of choice. Even though most of us find our wood at lumberyards rather than in forests and use power tools with jigs and fixtures in lieu of freehand work, these sawing and slicing tools are still very much a part of traditional woodworking practice.

Today, the average woodshop is crammed with power equipment—table saw, radial-arm saw, portable circular saw, saber saw. Nevertheless, there are times when only a traditional handsaw will do. A sharp, well-tuned handsaw is a pleasure to use. And the pleasure is all the greater if the saw has a beautifully shaped, decorative handle that fits your grip like a glove. The lovely designs engraved on the blades of many an early handsaw, as well as the fancy brass rivets or bronze escutcheons that secure their handles, further increase the pleasure of beholding—and holding—a vintage handsaw.

This chapter begins with all sorts of saws that were used by carpenters and cabinetmakers to rip and crosscut planks, cut joints, and saw out curved parts as well (logging saws are not included). The most common handsaws are panel saws with teeth shaped either for crosscut or ripping. The blades of the best saws were made of spring steel.

Another type of handsaw that still finds use in the modern shop is the backsaw. Backsaws have a stiffening steel or brass spine strip for reinforcement and are useful for cutting miters (using an old-fashioned miter box) or for sawing tenons, dovetails, and other joinery. Yet a third style of tool is the stair saw, which features a thin blade set in a wood handle that gives it full sup-port. Used primarily for cutting the sides of dadoes into the stair stringers that support the treads and risers, this small saw could also come in handy for sawing the female portion of a sliding dovetail joint.

Bowsaws, used to cut out all manner of woodwork, usually had blades ranging in length from 6 in. to 36 in. and in width anywhere from 1/8 in. or less to 1 in. or more. To keep the thin blade taut and prevent it from buckling during cutting, the frame is designed to tension the blade with a twist-tightened string (some saws used a threaded rod and wing nut). A stick called a toggle threaded between the bowstring strands give the user leverage for tightening the string.

The blades are typically held in place by slotted fittings on the ends of the handles that allow the user to rotate the blade during cutting, so tricky curvaceous patterns can be cut out without having to do a jig-step around the workpiece!

Edge tools have a long and interesting history. Axes, adzes, and chisels are among the most basic and primitive implements in the repertoire of early man. First made with blades fashioned from stones, these tools were flake sharpened from chunks of flint and obsidian. With the advent of metallurgy, they were manufactured from copper, bronze, and ultimetly from modern iron and steel.

Early axes made for woodworking performed a wide range of duties and were indispensable in the building trades. Felling axes were used to chop down trees and strip the trunk of branches. They could also split a trunk into planks or firewood, and the poll of a single-bit ax could be used for driving wedges. With their chisel-beveled edges, broadaxes were used to hew and dress beams, rafters, and girders for the construction of barns, houses, and other structures.

As carpenters from many parts of Europe, Asia, and the Americas employed hewn timbers in the construction of their buildings, broadax heads were made in endless variations that were as distinctive as the language and culture of the people who used them. The remarkable shapes of the blades of some of these axes, such as the goosewing hewing axes on p. 113, is sculpture in itself. A trained eye can distinguish one pattern from another and often tell you in what part of the world the ax originated.

The axes shown in this chapter represent only a small subsection of all the different special types that proliferated when most wooden items of the built world were constructed by specialized artisans, such as the shipwright, the cooper, and the coachmaker. And I've included one ax that's only marginally from the woodworking trades: a "boarding ax" (see p. 111) that was used for routine ship carpentry tasks, as well as for more grisly duties in the heat of battle.

A first cousin of the ax, the adze is a basic edged tool that has often had the misfortune of being described as "primitive" (especially by 19th-century anthropologists). Quite the contrary, an adze is a sophisticated and most versatile tool. In the hands of a skilled craftsman, it can accurately shape furniture parts and hollow out all manner of wooden forms from bowls to chair seats to canoes.

No less versatile is the chisel, another simple tool that will thanklessly tackle sundry paring tasks, trim delicate joinery, or chop out the largest angled mortise. Chisels are usually plain, but some have decorations bestowed upon them. Toward the end of this chapter you will find a couple of remarkable chisels with carved and decorated handles. ※

Chest of handsaws

These six handsaws are some of the better makes and models made in the past 150 years. At front right, an Atkins Perfection No. 53 with a damaskeened spring-steel blade and a fancy handle, typical of what they put on their better saws. At front left, an Atkins No. 400 saw with a rosewood handle and a "silver steel" spring-steel blade, the best that the company sold. At middle right, an Imperial saw, made in the mid-1800s and sold at St. Louis Hardware and Cutlery Co. The blade has a nib, and fancy rivets hold the handle in place. At middle left, a Simmonds Manufacturing Co. No. 8 patented 18-in. handsaw. At back right, a Disston D8 early ripsaw with a hole for an extra finger (detail, p. 100); Finally, at back left, an early Disston London spring-steel saw.

From the collection of Don Rosebrook

Tillotson and Taylor fancy handsaws

While the wood handles and steel blades are likely the same as were fitted to more ordinary saw models, the fancy bronze escutcheons with floral decorations in deep relief make these tools unusual and extraordinary. Both saws were made in Sheffield, England, and both are 10-point crosscut saws. The saw in the foreground was made by Thos. Tillotson; the saw in the background was made by the Taylor Brothers. Taylor was one of the more prolific handsaw manufacturers during the mid-19th century, when these saws were probably made.

From the collection of Patrick and Lisa Leach

DISSTON: THE FIRST AMERICAN HANDSAW MANUFACTURER

In the early 19th century, few American toolmakers manufactured handsaws; practically all handsaws were made in England. Hence, the English had a lock on the handsaw market in America until about 1860, when the Morrill Act placed a large tariff on foreign iron and steel imports, making English metal tools more expensive.

Established in 1840 in Philadelphia, Henry Disston built the first crucible cast-steel melting plant In 1855. After adding a rolling mill for steel plate in 1862, Disston become the first major saw manufacturer in America to produce saws successfully from its own iron and steel. The earliest saws manufactured by Henry Disston bear his name alone (see the brass-backed handsaw from the David Kretchun collection in the photo below). In 1865, Disston took his son, Hamilton, as a partner, and more of his sons joined in the family business later. He also added a square and level shop in partnership with his brother-in-law, Joab Morss (see the top photo on p. 25).

Disston ripsaw

The tiger-maple handle on this Disston ripsaw is both attractive and extremely practical. The extra hole above the grip allows users to hook a thumb through, for more power and less fatigue when taking a long rip cut through a thick plank. The handle is designed for a right-handed user.

Collection of Ronald W. Pearson, D.O.

User-made rosewood bowsaw

Hanging on a wall with vintage tools, this handsome
rosewood bowsaw was crafted by Dr. Larry Robinson,
a contemporary emergency-room surgeon. Robinson
made and French-polished the saw's frame and
tensioning crossbar. He also made the blade to see if he
could improve on what was available commercially. It's
rumored that he wasn't entirely happy with the results
and sold the saw to a collector friend who admired its
graceful look.

From the collection of Valdis Petersons

Panther handsaw

One of the most interesting handsaws ever manufactured was the Panther saw, so named for the snarling beast on the leading edge of the blond wood handle (detail, below). The saw was made by Woodrough & McParlin Saw Co., Cincinnati, Ohio, from London spring steel; the one shown here has a 12-point blade. The company operated from 1856 to 1890, at which time it was bought out by Henry Disston and Sons. Although Woodrough & McParlin made an entire line of handsaws (and probably mill saws), the carved handle on the Panther was unique and is highly sought after by collectors today.

From the collection of George Gaspari

WHY AREN'T THERE MORE OLD HANDSAWS AROUND?

While countless handplanes have survived the vicissitudes of time—and the whims of uncaring owners—for generations, it's uncommon to see handsaws that are much more than a hundred years old. Why?

Compared to other tools, the manufacture of handsaw blades was technically complex: Heavy, expensive equipment and highly specialized craftstmanship were necessary to produce a blade that had the right balance of hardness, stiffness, and flexibility. Hence, early sawblades were very costly to make and scarce, so they were expensive to purchase. To get the most out of a handsaw, generations of owners would sharpen it down to a point where it was too narrow to use. Even then, the expensive steel wasn't wasted: an old blade was cut up and made into hand scrapers. Old handsaws were simply used up entirely!

Half-backed handsaws

When a short handsaw was needed that didn't require the rigidity of a full brass back, a half-backed handsaw was ideal. The short brass spine, such as on the early Henry Disston saw in the background, added rigidity, yet allowed a deeper, less restricted cut. For saws as well as other tools, some owners preferred to make their own handles. The exceptionally fancy handle in the foreground is sized and drilled to replace a similarly sized stock handle.

From the collection of Bill Phillips

Carved swanhead bowsaw

With its rosewood frame, octagonal ebony handles, and frame tips carved as a pair of long-necked swans, this saw must have been destined for some fine work indeed. The saw's frame, which holds a 10-in.-long blade, is stamped only with the owner's name: G. Pirie.

From the collection of Roger B. Phillips

Disston multi-purpose handsaw

With ruled markings along the top edge of its blade and a pair of level vials and a square built into the handle, this Disston & Sons handsaw did a lot more than just saw wood. A user could measure a board, mark it for a square cut, and even level it during installation. Even if the extra tools weren't used daily, they could certainly come in handy on occasions when the user's tool chest was out of reach.

From the collection of Bill Phillips

Pride of the Road handsaw

With its fancy graphic engraving of a horse-drawn carriage, this Pride of the Road handsaw is only about 10 in. long and small enough for the hand of a child. However, the curved sawblade is best adapted to starting cuts in the middle of a board, say for flooring repairs.

Collection of Roger K. Smith

D-handle dovetail saw

This early European tool with a user-made walnut D-handle is very similar to the more modern stair saw, a tool used primarily for cutting the sides of the dadoes into stair stringers for the treads and risers. However, the crudely filed blade on this particular tool has large teeth that lack set, indicating that it was probably used for cuts with the grain, such as for ripping rabbet joints or cutting slots for sliding dovetails.

From the collection of Roger B. Phillips

Disston saw-setting model and Vulcan saw

This 6-in.-long sterling-silver saw, patented by Henry Disston in 1920, is a guide for setting and filing handsaw teeth. The model has samples of teeth cut at 5, 6, 8, 10 and 12 points per inch. The model sits atop an unusual handsaw made by Vulcan, which has its wooden handle secured to the blade with bent copper fittings.

From the collection of Don Rosebrook

Two fancy bowsaws

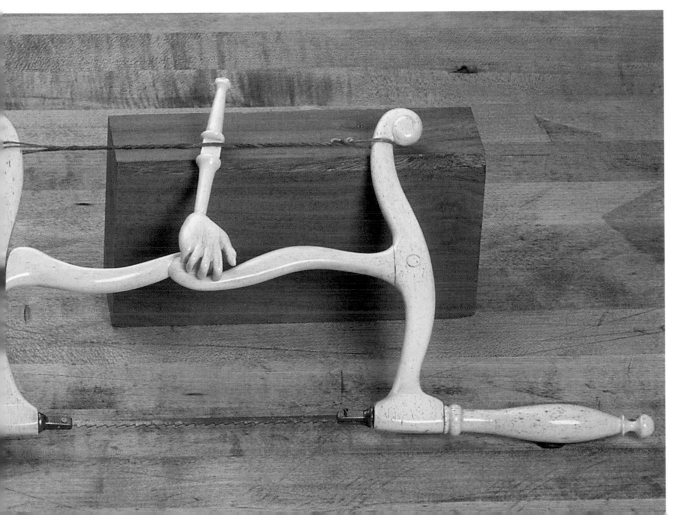

These two petite bowsaws were likely made as presentation tools or gifts (neither shows signs of appreciable wear). The use of whalebone suggests that they were made by a seaman, possibly to pass the time during a long voyage. The saw at near left is made entirely of whalebone, its curvaceous frame with scrolled tips and brace supporting a 6-in. blade. The lever used to wind the tensioning cord ends in a whimsically carved hand. The saw at far left has a Gabon ebony frame fitted with a 4½-in.-long blade. Its handles are fashioned from whalebone.

From the collection of Roger B. Phillips

Pennsylvania Dutch broadaxes

These Pennsylvania Dutch axes are European in style, mimicking patterns that were produced for hundreds of years. Despite the adherence to tradition, the maker of these two axes added his own unique touch that's as recognizable as a signature: the ogee curve at the heel end of both blades.

From the collection of Bill Phillips

The touchmarks found on early European axes, such as the German goosewing ax in the photo at right, from the collection of Ronald W. Pearson, D.O., were impressed by the blade's maker possibly as a signature or to specify where (and possibly when) the tool was made. Unfortunately, the key to understanding the meaning of these marks has long since been lost, making such marks more of an interesting decoration than a source of information.

Not all of these axes were used in the building trades. It is speculated, for instance, that axes with three holes punched through the blade—a touchmark pattern seen on some old German and Austrian broadaxes—may once have been wielded by an executioner for beheading condemned prisoners.

European goosewing ax

Looking more like a weapon than a tool for slicing wood, this Austrian goosewing ax has a hooked tip, probably more as an expression of the design sense of the maker than for any useful purpose.

From the collection of John and Janet Wells

Early French ax

While this French-style ax obviously was forged by a highly skilled craftsman, its identifying markings are minimal (it bears the initials "G. S." and a date: 1613). It appears to have its original handle (or at least an early replacement), hewn from elm wood. The delicate scrolls that adorn the head were punched and twisted out of the billet of iron that makes up the head itself.

From the collection of Roger B. Phillips

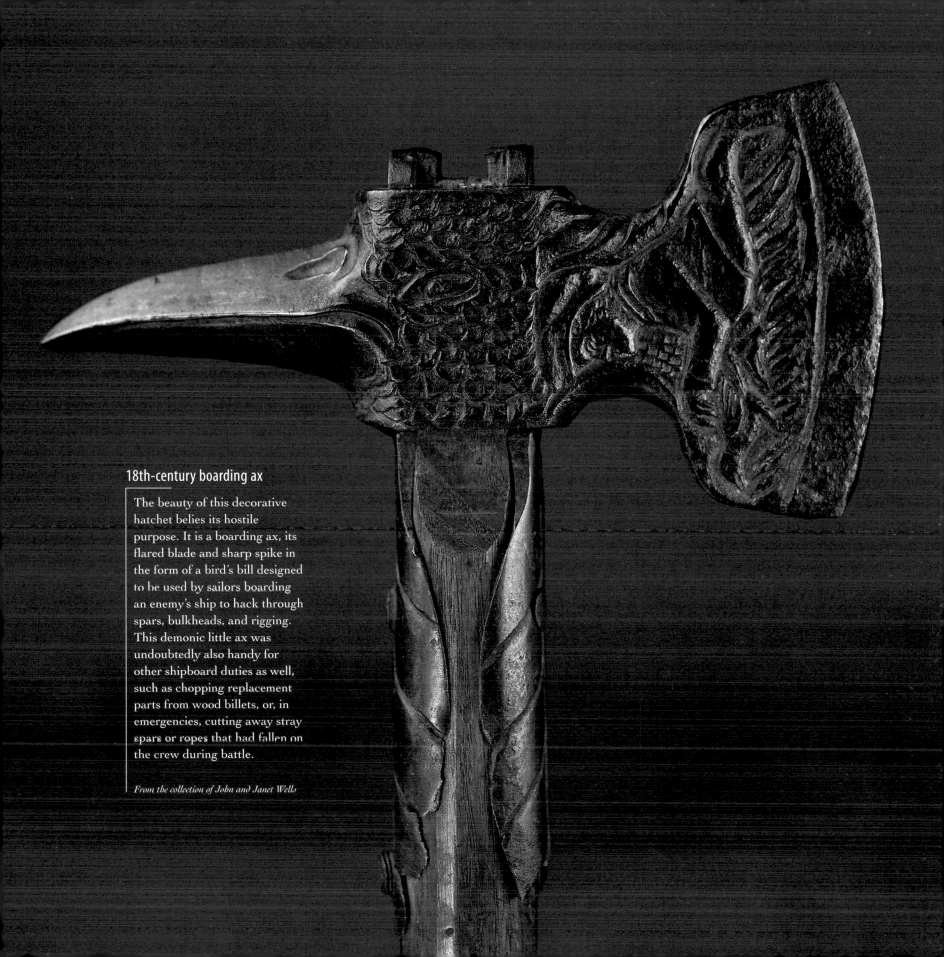

18th-century boarding ax

The beauty of this decorative hatchet belies its hostile purpose. It is a boarding ax, its flared blade and sharp spike in the form of a bird's bill designed to be used by sailors boarding an enemy's ship to hack through spars, bulkheads, and rigging. This demonic little ax was undoubtedly also handy for other shipboard duties as well, such as chopping replacement parts from wood billets, or, in emergencies, cutting away stray spars or ropes that had fallen on the crew during battle.

From the collection of John and Janet Wells

Like their ancient relative the broadax, modern axes come in innumerable sizes and style of head (a knowledgeable ax collector can tell you the name of an ax pattern by the shape and style of its head). Here are three different axes, made for different purposes. As their distinctive embossed trademarks show, they are all the same brand: Black Raven tools, made by the Kelly Axe and Tool Works, in Charleston, West Virgina. At left is a double-bit ax, a stout tool for felling a tree. Its two edges gave the feller twice as much time between sharpenings. At right is a hatchet, which was known as a camping ax or hunting ax. This tool was handy for chopping up branches, splitting small logs for firewood, or shaving kindling. At center is a shingling hatchet. It combines a flared bit for splitting roofing shingles or shakes with a long hammering poll and a nail-pulling notch on the side of the bit. Although the tools aren't very different at all from their contemporary counterparts, these Black Raven axes, from the collection of Bud Steere, date from the early decades of this century.

Goosewing axes

These early German-style goosewing axes have beautifully shaped heads that bear an elaborate pattern of decorative punchmarks. Their original handles are bent to one side (usually the right) to protect the fingers of the user while hewing a log or plank. Such axes were often brought to America by German immigrants, many of whom moved to Pennsylvania prior to the mid-1800s.

From the collection of Bud Steere

Rosewood-handled chisels

Although the tools lack fancy ornamentation, the clean, simple lines of this set of user-made chisels, stored in a leather tool roll, make them classics. The rosewood handles are sized and shaped to fit the hand comfortably and feel as sturdy as can be.

From the collection of Bill Phillips

Pascal chisel with carved handle

Surrounded by other decorative tools, this chisel is part of the Pascal collection of decorative tools at the Canadian Museum of Civilization in Ottawa, Ontario (see p. 169). Its ornately carved handle gives it a sculptural feel, though it's doubtful that the shape is very comfortable to hold.

Courtesy of Lee Valley Tools

Don Quixote hand adze

This boxwood hand adze made by English toolmaker and miniaturist David Brookshaw is a scale reproduction of a famous 18th-century tool resembling a rider atop a horse. It's thought to be based on the Cervantes character Don Quixote, with the suggestion of sails and cogs from a windmill decorating the handle. Hand adzes were commonly used for hewing down rough surfaces or for scooping out forms, such as bowls or chair seats.

Collection of Ronald W. Pearson, D.O.

Northwest Coast D-adze

The Tlingit, Kwakiutl, and Haida tribes of the Pacific Northwest Coast developed a highly refined art for decoratively carving their functional and ceremonial wares. Despite the sophistication of the work, the woodworking tools are simple. One such tool is the D-handled adze, which is terrific for hollowing out a canoe or serving bowl or for roughing out a sculptural house post or totem pole.

From the collection of Steven F. Dice

Bone-handled gouge

One can only hope that this fishtailed gouge, with its ornately chip-carved whalebone handle and brass details, was part of a full set of carving chisels that one of us will find someday at a flea market. Most likely European, the gouge is dated 1671 and has initials engraved in the butt end of its handle.

Courtesy of Lee Valley Tools

TOOL TREASURES
OF THE ORIENT

The woodworking tools developed in the Far East were inspired by a very different culture from the European traditions that spawned the tools we're familiar with in the West. Japanese saws that cut on the pull stroke and Chinese planes with odd side handles that are pushed represent an entirely different approach to woodworking than most Westerners are accustomed to. But it is an approach that in recent years has attracted a considerable number of American converts.

Despite their simple appearances, Japanese tools have subtle qualities and an elegance that, to my eyes at least, are no less remarkable than the ornate "eye candy" proffered by decorative Western tools. Simple adornments, such as the acid-etched surface of a forged chisel or plane blade and the patterned cane wrapping on a saw handle, may be understated and unobtrusive, but such is the Japanese approach to the decorative arts, an ap-

proach that is seamlessly integrated with Japanese religion and philosophies of life. And the elegance of Japanese tools extends far into their functional design as well. For example, an old-style Japanese handplane blade is tapered lengthwise. It seats into a tapered slot, so that tapping the blade into the body forces the blade tighter in the slot. By contrast, Western planes have flat blades that require a separate wedge to hold them in place.

Another remarkable aspect of Japanese tools is how they are made. Finer tools are made by highly trained artisans, the best of whom have achieved the status of masters of their trade. The art of such small-shop craftsmen is hard earned and much revered. The best-quality tools come with their own cases, crafted in the traditional manner from paulownia, a blond wood with silver-gray streaks that is treasured by Japanese cabinetmakers and craftsmen. The cases

have lovely ink calligraphy and chop marks (marks from an engraved signet block) that identify not only the name and status of the maker, but often the "name" of the tool itself. Special, one-of-a-kind tools made by master craftsmen are often given a unique identity and moniker—see, for example, the "Evening Calm on Awaji Island" plane, shown at left in the photo on p. 123.

It is thought that the tools of Japan share a common ancestry with those of China, though in many cases, the toolmaking traditions have diverged significantly. They share the use of flexible squares and ink lines, and Chinese handplanes have simple wooden bodies just as Japanese planes do. But Chinese planes are pushed rather than pulled and have side handles to accommodate the practice,

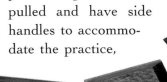

a feature incorporated into the handplanes made throughout Indonesia and other parts of the South Pacific.

Unfortunately, very little has been passed down in the way of information about Chinese woodworking practices. Scholars are even uncertain of the traditional Chinese names for many of the tools found in a basic toolkit! Why is so little known? Probably because in China, cabinetmakers were considered artisans but not artists. Other than stories of legendary figures, such as P'an Ku and Lu Pan (considered to be the first Chinese carpenters), there is literally no mention of noteworthy cabinetmakers for the entire history of the classic Chinese dynasties. Because these makers have remained anonymous, all we know of their tools or how they used them is witnessed by examples of their excellent work (see Robert Ellsworth's great volume, *Chinese Furniture* (Random House, 1971).

While most of the tools shown in *The Art of Fine Tools* are 100 years of age or older and can be called antiques, most of the tools in this chapter were made in recent decades, and some are nearly brand new. Partly, this is because it is only in the past few decades that Asian-style tools have gained acceptance among American woodworkers. Unlike European vintage tools that are imported by dealers in great numbers and bought by collectors at auction, fine Asian tools are scarce in the United States; most are still in their native countries. Perhaps because of their appearance of simplicity, Asian tools have not yet caught on with Western tool collectors to the extent that fancier vintage tools from Europe or North America have.

The collection of Asian woodworking tools presented in this chapter is selected entirely from collections in the United States. Nonetheless, these tools represent the finest traditions of Asian toolmaking, including one small handplane that was made in India. Only a few simple Chinese tools are included. Featured instead are tools made in Indonesia and Malaysia, countries that adopted basic Chinese tools but made them more colorful and ornate. I hope that the visual and functional qualities embodied in these tools will serve as a counterpoint to the Western perspective that prevails in the rest of this book and provide a more comprehensive look at the many facets of the toolmaker's art worldwide. ✳

119

Japanese smoothing plane and box

The highest-quality Japanese handplanes, such as the *horyu* (Treasure of the Dragon) smoothing plane shown here, have their own fitted wood boxes, usually made of *kiri* (paulownia). Characters painted on the box using traditional brushed calligraphy show the name of the maker, in this case Japanese master Masao Miyamoto, and sometimes inspirational thoughts or sayings. The body of this plane (called a *dai*) is made from *akagashi* (Japanese red oak), the strongest and most durable of all Japanese wood species. The blanks for the best *dai* are split out of logs so that they contain the straightest grain. Note the remarkable figure on the end grain of the smoothing plane shown here; it is part of what makes this such a highly prized plane. In addition to strength, oak is a great choice for wood-bodied planes because it has enough flexibility to keep the blade in place by friction alone: The blade is set and adjusted by tapping it in place with a small hammer. The crescent-shaped areas inlaid into the edges of the tool's laminated blade are tapping surfaces of harder steel. To remove the blade (or decrease the depth of cut), the back end of the plane body is tapped with the hammer.

From the collection of Curtis Bowden

Japanese smoothing plane in action

Designed to be pulled instead of pushed, a Japanese plane has only a few parts: a wood body, a blade, and a chipbreaker. But its simplicity belies its ability to perform: In skillful hands, a well-tuned, high-quality Japanese smoothing plane, such as this *kenkon* (Spirit of the Sword) plane, made by master blade smith Usui, can easily create yards-long, paper-thin shavings the width of the blade.

Courtesy of the Japan Woodworker Catalog

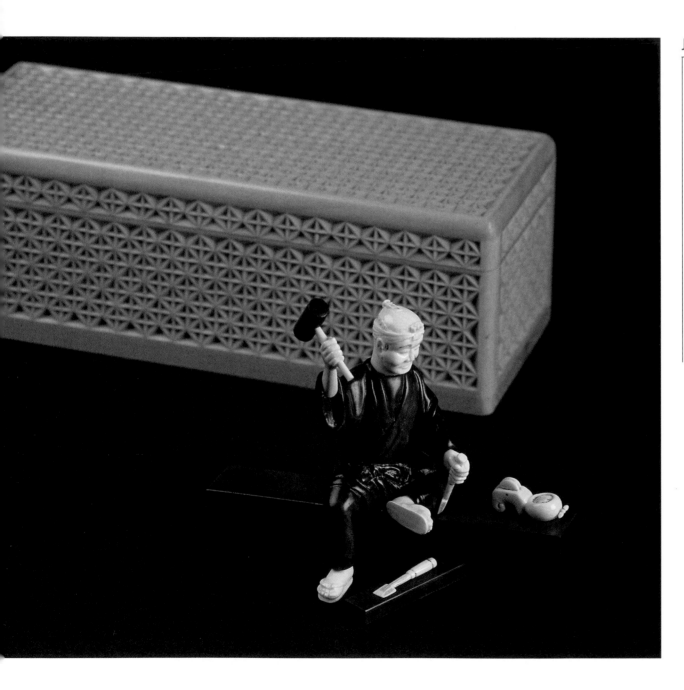

Japanese carpenter figure

Depicting a traditional Japanese carpenter, this carving is a reproduction of an original figurine, 8½ in. tall, which sold at the 1995 International Tool Auction for £4650. Carved in boxwood and ivory by toolmaker and miniaturist David Brookshaw, of Loughborough, England, the carpenter figure is using a chisel and mallet to chop a mortise in the beam he is sitting on. His *sumitsubo* (Japanese ink line), which was used to lay out the joint, is sitting beside him.

Collection of Ronald W. Pearson, D.O.

To the traditional Japanese *shokunin* (craftsman), a chisel or plane blade is far more than a simple piece of sharpened steel. It is a tool that has an individual identity and a personality that transcends its mere utilitarian function. This quotation from Toshio Odate's excellent book, *Japanese Woodworking Tools: Their Tradition, Spirit and Use* (The Taunton Press, 1984), serves to illustrate this point:

"…the quality of a blade is much more than how well it will cut. True quality also concerns itself with attitude and motivation….A blade forged by a young blacksmith may be both beautiful and have a good cutting edge, yet its beauty in part is derived from the creator's youth and physical vitality. A truly high-quality blade is forged out of maturity: physical vitality tempered with spiritual calm, sharpness balanced with serenity. In short, the blade forged by the mature blacksmith is the blade that reflects a more complex interplay of the inner, emotional life."

When Japan's civil-war period ended around the turn of the 17th century, the same blacksmiths who had forged samurai swords began to apply their highly refined skills to the making of farm implements and woodworking tools, literally turning from swords to plowshares and chisels and plane blades.

Both of the decoratively finished plane blades in these Japanese smooth planes were made in traditional fashion: by forge-welding a hard-steel cutting edge to shock-absorbing mild steel obtained from an old ship anchor chain. Master blade maker Chiyozuru Sadahide's Evening Calm on Awaji Island plane is shown at right; the plane at far right is by Masao Miyamoto (see p. 120).

Courtesy of the Japan Woodworker Catalog

Four Japanese chisels

The tools shown on the facing page exemplify four different blade-making processes and their resulting finishes. Far left: A paring chisel with an "ink pattern blade" made by the sword lamination process. The *jigane* (the soft-steel body of the chisel to which is forge-welded a hard-steel blade edge) is made by forging then folding two different types of steel, creating many thin, strong layers. Center left: A bench chisel made by laminating together *yasuki* (blue steel) and *kamaji* wrought iron, a special iron salvaged from old ship anchors, boilers, and bridge girders. This chisel's handle, which has a hammered iron hoop, is turned from a white oak branch. Center right: A paring chisel, made by the same process used to create samurai swords. Wrought iron is forge-welded to high-carbon white steel. The blades are hand-hammered at low temperatures to strengthen and toughen the edge, leaving a pattern of hammer marks on the surface. Right: a socket slick with the *mokume* pattern, a result of forge-welding blue steel to old wrought iron, then folding the layers together repeatedly. The surface of the resulting blade is then etched with acid, which exposes the layered structure. The slick's handle is made from Japanese red sandalwood.

Courtesy of the Japan Woodworker Catalog

Japanese paring chisel

The Japanese paring chisel *(tsuki-nomi)* has been used for hundreds of years by carpenters for smoothing the cheeks of large tenons and for cleaning up deep mortises used for traditional house-frame construction. Like the Western socket slick, this tool has a long handle that can be grasped and pushed with both hands for added leverage during heavy cuts in large timbers. The bevel angle of the blade is low, making for a very sharp edge that pushes through stock more easily than a blade with a high-angle bevel.

From the collection of Curtis Bowden

Japanese-chisel design

Most modern Japanese chisels incorporate the best features of both socket and tang-style chisels: The end of the metal blade terminates in a heavy tang that fits into a recess in the handle. Additional reinforcement is provided by a tapered metal ferrule that matches the taper of the rear portion of the blade and fits over the tapered end of the wood handle. Like the metal socket, the ferrule compresses the wood handle over the area where the tang is inserted and expands the wood outward; it's a very strong arrangement. The striking end of the chisel is reinforced with a steel hoop, or *sagariwa*. The hoops on the chisels shown here bear decorative facets from the hammer strikes used to shape them.

From the collection of Curtis Bowden

Twisted-handle Japanese chisels

Although his shop employs assembly-line procedures and is equipped with some modern machinery, master chisel maker Iyoroi produces tools using traditional methods, crafting each individually. This special set of presentation chisels, each with an unusual twisted shank, was made for Fred Damsen, tool collector and owner of The Japan Woodworker in Alameda, California.

Courtesy of the Japan Woodworker Catalog

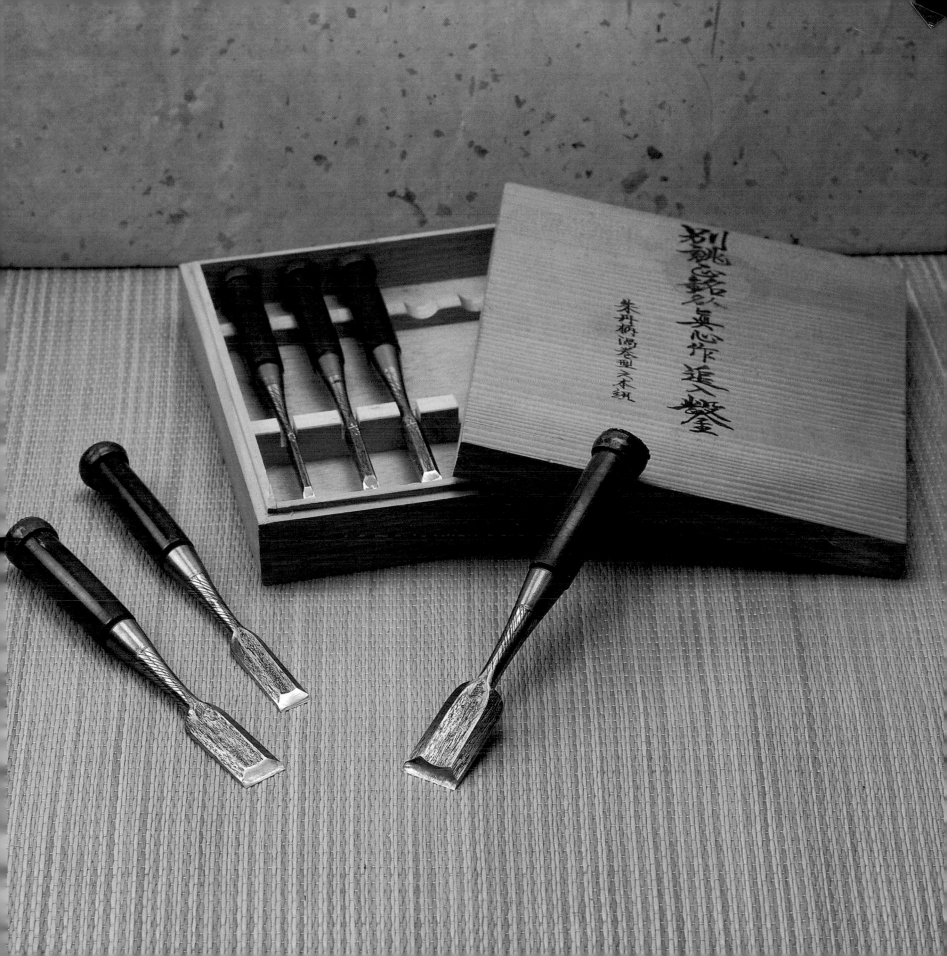

Japanese saws

They may look simple, but these two Japanese handsaws *(noko giri)* represent the finest of Japan's toolmaking arts. The double-purpose *ryoba* saw in the foreground has two rows of teeth: One side is for ripping, the other for crosscutting (detail, p. 130). This tool, made by the saw- and samurai-sword-making master Tetsunosuke Miyano, is valued at over $15,000 (and that's without a handle!). The handle in the foreground is made of wood wrapped with sharkskin, a traditional covering. In the background is a *dozuki* saw, a steel-backed thin-blade crosscut saw with small, razor-sharp teeth designed for fine miter cuts and for cutting joints such as dovetails. To give the user a better grip, its wood handle is covered with a decorative pattern of wrapped cane.

Courtesy of the Japan Woodworker Catalog

THE ADVANTAGES OF
PULLING VS. PUSHING A SAW

Japanese saws, such as the *dozuki* or *ryoba,* are made to cut on the pull stroke. Why? to find out, take a strip of plain paper, hold one end firmly, and pinch the other. Pull the strip between pinched fingers; this represents a sawblade being drawn through a kerf in the wood. The paper remains straight and taut. The Japanese blade can be very thin, so it removes less wood (and thus requires less effort to power through a cut) than a thicker blade would. Why have a thicker blade? Just try to push that strip of paper between your pinched fingers. This is just like using a panel saw that must cut on the push stroke; the blade must be thicker to resist buckling in the cut, and so it removes a thicker kerf, requiring more driving power.

Like everything else in life, using a Japanese saw correctly takes practice. The teeth and blade body are relatively delicate, especially on fine-tooth *dozuki* saws. But once you get the hang of it, my guess is that you'd be loathe to go back to pushing a standard Western-style panel saw.

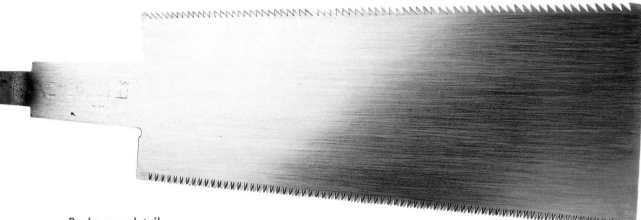

Ryoba saw, detail

In this photo of the master saw maker Tetsunosuke Miyano's prized *ryoba* saw, you can clearly see the marks of his labor. The streaks on the blade are formed by the master scraping the blade to final thickness. For optimum performance, the blade must be carefully scraped to different thicknesses at both edges and ends. In contrast, a modern production saw is thicknessed with abrasive machinery—it's a quicker method that produces serviceable results at a lower cost.

Courtesy of the Japan Woodworker Catalog

Box for *ryoba* saw, underside of lid

The inside of the lid of the paulownia box that houses the *ryoba* saw seen in the photo on p. 128 bears calligraphic writing identifying the tool as the work of Tetsunosuke Miyano. No less important are the two red chop marks: The top one signifies that he is a master saw maker, the lower that he is a master samurai sword maker.

Courtesy of the Japan Woodworker Catalog

Fancy *sumitsubo*

Existing in its present form since the 14th century A.D., the *sumitsubo* is the Japanese equivalent of the American chalk line. Its thin ink-soaked line is used for marking straight lines on long boards and panels, typically to guide ripping and resawing (skilled Japanese carpenters can even strike subtly curved lines by pulling back and snapping the line at an angle). When a temple or shrine is built, it is an old Japanese custom to give an elaborately made *sumitsubo,* such as this large oak tool with a carved turtle perched over its ink bowl, to the master carpenter at the completion of construction.

From the collection of Roger B. Phillips

TOOLS OF THE *SHOKUNIN*

In the ancient Japanese tradition, the skilled woodworker is called a *shokunin,* a word whose literal translation is "artisan" or "craftsman." The *shokunin*'s skill is acquired through many years of apprenticeship (which in traditional Japan began at the age of eight or nine; only boys were apprenticed). But according to the well-known craftsman and *shoji* screen maker Toshio Odate, the word *shokunin* has a much deeper meaning: "*Shokunin* means not only having technical skill, but also implies an attitude and social consciousness…a social obligation to work his best for the general welfare of the people, [an] obligation both material and spiritual."

It's not difficult to understand why a *shokunin*'s tools are greatly prized and deeply respected—such tools are not to be used by untrained people. Traditionally, *shokunin* celebrated their tools annually on New Year's Day. The cleaned and sharpened tools are placed in their toolboxes and arranged in a special decorated area still found in many Japanese shops and homes, known as the *tokonoma*. As a gesture of thanks for the hard work the tools perform in the life and vocation of the *shokunin*, each toolbox is covered with a sheet of rice paper, on which are placed two rice cakes and a tangerine—symbols of prosperity and the richness of life.

Balinese ink line

This ink line *(sepat)* from Bali has a face carved in the likeness of Bhoma, the spirit of the forest. On the predominantly Hindu island of Bali, the Bhoma is often carved above the doorways of temples, a symbol of the sanctuary within. This ink line is carved from the hibiscus wood indigenous to Indonesia (not the same kind of hibiscus that's an ornamental flowering shrub in Western gardens). To use the *sepat*, the *sang ging* (traditional Balinese house builder or woodworker) creates a dye by burning candlenut, then grinding it into a sticky paste.

From the collection of Roger B. Phillips

Carved *sumitsubo* and Japanese marking knife

Unlike many American craftsmen, who use pencil and chalk lines to mark cuts and joinery, Japanese craftsmen prefer to use ink for layout, as it produces thinner lines that promote tighter-tolerance work. Two contemporary examples of the traditional *sumitsubo* ink line are shown here. The one at right was carved from koa wood by Hawaiian craftsman Rick Hahn; the one at far right was carved by Japanese carpenter Hiroshi Morita from keyaki wood. Both tools have fine silk twine on their reels and cotton wadding saturated with dark ink contained in their bowls. There is also a simple tapered knife of the sort used by Japanese craftsmen for a wide variety of woodworking tasks, such as marking out joints, carving details, or whittling small parts. This knife's tool-steel blade has an ornate covering layer of copper with a surface that's decoratively hammer marked. The handle and scabbard are from Japanese pagoda wood *(Sohora japonica)* adorned with pearl inlays.

Courtesy of the Japan Woodworker Catalog

Chinese ruler and tools

The familiar Arabic numeral system is nowhere to be found on this early Chinese ruler, whose increments are marked in traditional pictographs rendered in ink. Accompanying the foot-long wood rule are two other traditional Chinese tools: a shoulder plane made from *hua li* (rosewood) and an ink line.

From the collection of Steven F. Dice

Sumitsubo, carved crane and turtle detail

This detail of Hiroshi Morita's hand-carved *sumitsubo* shows the turtle and crane motif that's commonly depicted on Japanese ink lines (the design is commonly rendered on inexpensive plastic *sumitsubo* made in Japan today). The wings of the crane encircle the bowl, while the turtle carries the world on his back.

Courtesy of the Japan Woodworker Catalog

Malaysian plane

Carved in the form of a man, this wood-bodied handplane was most likely made in Malaysia, carved from an unidentified indigenous species. The jack-plane-length tool is patterned after a traditional Chinese plane, with the carved figure's arms serving as side handles for pushing the plane through a cut.

From the collection of Clifford R. Sapienza

Indonesian plane with carved snakes

Made in Indonesia, this wooden bench plane has a pair of carved snakes intertwined at the front of the plane body. Paint ground from earth pigments adds color to the tool, while the decorative snakes form an unusual detail that's not for squeamish craftsmen.

From the collection of Clifford R. Sapienza

Dragon-faced plane

The plane shown below, which probably came originally from an Indonesian island, is decorated at the front with a carved depiction of a mythical timber-chewing beast of that region. The back end of the plane (detail, left) has a carved human face. Patterned after a traditional Chinese jack plane, this tool has rounded cross handles just behind the iron. Unlike the Japanese, who pulled their planes with the workpiece resting on the floor, craftsman in Indonesia worked as the Chinese do, on a bench top. They pushed their planes, using the handles for control and leverage. In this way, these planes work much like long-soled spokeshaves.

From the collection of Clifford R. Sapienza

Fancy block plane

This ornate little plane was probably made in India. The top of its exotic wood body is lavishly decorated with five fluted brass beads, and the sides have numerous applied brass ornaments and bone inlays. The 2½-in.-long, 2-in.-wide iron sole screwed to the bottom of the wood body is slightly convex in both directions, indicating that the plane was probably used for light hollowing or roughing out.

From the collection of Roger B. Phillips

Indonesian ink lines

These ink lines from one of the Indonesian islands (possibly Lombok) are decorated with odd creatures and mythological beasts, including Gadarba the flying lion, seen carved at the front of the tool at left. All three ink lines are carved from *sawo* wood, an indigenous species similar to mahogany. Like the traditional Japanese *sumitsubo,* these tools use an inked line to strike a mark over the length of a board or panel. A small reel with a crank in the midsection of each tool holds a length of thin twine (note the reel crank on the lower portion of the tool at right; it protrudes from the center of the wheel of a horse-drawn chariot). The twine line feeds through a small compartment that the craftsman fills with a wad of ink-soaked fiber. A small plug, carved as an attentively perched frog on each tool, caps the ink compartment. The line is fed through the body of the tool (it comes out the flying lion's mouth, left, and bird's mouth, center) and is attached to a small pin or loop for securing to the end of the work during marking; note the carved mask attached to the line on the middle tool.

From the collection of Roger B. Phillips

139

INGENIOUS 6 MECHANISMS AND MACHINES

The range of human ingenuity and innovation knows few boundaries. Although not as widely celebrated for their creations as scientists and artists, woodworkers and toolmakers have certainly come up with their share of groundbreaking achievements, creating the tools that fashion wood into the objects of our built world.

The quest to build a better mousetrap is an ongoing activity, and there's no stemming the tide of new tools and gadgets that announce themselves on the pages of every new woodworking catalog that gets crammed into your mailbox. But modern-day inventiveness pales in the face of what went on in the past few centuries, when a tidal wave of new developments and ingenious ideas affected virtually every aspect of material life. And woodworking, both as an industry and as an individual practice, certainly wasn't unaffected. Toolmakers, designers, craftsmen, and basement inventors alike conceived, concocted, and conjured up all types of clever contraptions that made woodworking tools easier to use, more accurate, and, in some cases, safer.

At a time when the major tool companies of the day—Stanley Rule & Level Company, Disston Saw, Sargent Tool— made major strides with their newest, grandest tools, there were also thousands of smaller companies bringing their ingenuity to market. Thousands of father-and-son toolmaking businesses were working out of garages all over America. These small firms not only prototyped their innovative tools, but often manufactured them (in hopes that their ideas would be purchased by one of the big tool companies for a princely sum).

Some tool inventors simply manufactured what they had dreamed up, so unconcerned with credit and fame that they didn't even stamp their name into their creations. But most did seek recognition and also assurance that their ideas would remain their own. They sought legal protection against those who might borrow or even steal their ideas for personal profit. Hence, most new tool ideas were patented.

Congress created the U.S. patent system with the Patent Act of 1790 in order to give Americans a way to document the ownership of ideas. The Patent Office has records for tools patented in America that extend back to 1836 (there were thousands of patents granted before then, but the Patent Office was destroyed in an infamous fire in 1836 and all of the records were lost). Many of the patents for early American-made woodworking tools, such as bit braces and handplanes, were for tools that came as replacements for expensive tools then being imported from abroad, mostly from England.

The first part of this chapter explores a small number of examples of some of the more noteworthy tool innovations of the last century. Some of these demonstrate the inventor's ability to take a basic idea and used it in a novel way: For example, the Fuller's level (see the photo on p. 150) employs a plumb bob inside an adjustable arm, thereby transforming it into an accurate inclinometer. Other examples show special tools that were invented in response to specific needs: C. Bede invented the "electric level" (see the bottom photo on p. 152) to provide a means of seeing the bubble vial clearly when working on a dimly lit job site, such as when putting up support beams in a mine shaft.

No aspect or component of a tool is ever exempt from improvement, and 19th-century toolmakers sought better ways of doing just about everything. Consider, for instance, the countless different mechanisms for setting and adjusting a plane iron. Some tool designs are notable, not because they work so well, but because they accomplish a relatively simple task in a remarkably complicated way, such as the ivory-geared plow plane shown on pp. 142-143. Even if such designs have not survived the test of time, it's fun to look back and admire their ingenuity, no matter how misguided.

The second part of this chapter takes up another popular area of inventors' interest: combination tools. Maybe it's the survivalist in us, or some kind of primitive desire to be the master of all situations, that makes us yearn for a single tool that can perform a variety of functions (after all, isn't the Swiss Army knife the single most popular tool in the world?). Some of the devices shown combine tools that logically belong together in order to perform a multi-step task, for example, opening a wood crate and then later nailing it shut. Other combinations are more dubious. These fairly strange cross-pollinations include such oddities as a combination hammer with a handplane or crosscut saw and level all in the same tool.

The chapter concludes with one of the grandest examples of innovation in vintage tool design: the ornamental turning lathe. Although this book deals primarily in hand tools, I felt that no chapter on ingenious tools and mechanisms could fail to acknowledge these remarkably engineered human-powered machine tools. These lathes, driven by a foot treadle alone, could accomplish complicated and beautiful decorative work that almost defies the imagination.

In their heyday, Holtzapffel and other ornamental-lathe manufacturers provided artistic outlet and amusement for many a well-heeled member of the gentry (ornamental lathes were always expensive machines). Ornamental turning was a favorite activity for European royalty, including Wilhelm III, King of the Netherlands, Archduke Otto von Hapsburg of Austria, and even Queen Victoria of England (though I find it hard to imagine a lady of her statuesque grandeur donning an apron and face shield to indulge in this noble pastime). ✄

Self-adjusting plow plane with ivory gears

The gear train on this rosewood and ivory self-adjusting plow plane (detail, facing page) certainly earns it the Rube Goldberg award for most complicated way of accomplishing a relatively simple task—setting the distance between the plane's fence and the blade. Made by the Ohio Tool Company of Columbus, Ohio, this plane has a silver sole plate and a silver-plated skate. A silver pointer (atop the fence between the arms) indicates the distance between the fence and blade on a curved scale of inlaid ivory. The plane, from the Cliff Brown collection, fairly bristles with decorative silver plaques in the form of a star, eagles, and even Lady Liberty (seen at the front, below the plaque that bears the maker's name). A plaque alongside the gears on top is inscribed: "J.A. Montgomery—Foreman; 1857." Montgomery was presented with this plane in recognition of his 14 years of faithful service to the Ohio Tool Company.

Courtesy Roger K. Smith, Patented Transitional & Metallic Planes In America, Vol II; *(photos by Joseph Szaszfai)*

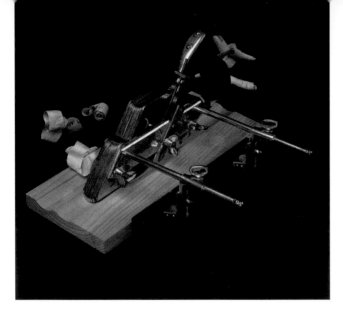

Walker Patent molding plow plane

Made in about 1885 by the Walker Tool Company of Erie, Pennsylvania, the Walker Adjustable Face Plane offered another approach to replacing the tremendous number of different planes—plows, dadoes, rabbets, filletsters, side beads, sash, and so on—commonly employed by woodworkers of the day. The Walker has a unique sole composed of six separate metal plates held between the frame sides of the plane body. Loosening a pair of wing nuts allowed the user to reconfigure the sole to match more closely the shape of the cutter that had been fitted: concave, convex, ogee, or stepped. Cutters themselves were shaped on both ends, so the overall number of cutters in a set could be reduced to half. The nickel-plated tool's plow-style fence can be mounted on either side of the blade for greater versatility. The Walker came complete with a neat wooden box and a set of 30 dual-profile cutters for $12.50, then a princely sum.

Mel Miller Collection

Bailey block plane

The novel corrugations cast into the bottom of the nearly 7½-in.-long Bailey Tool Co. No. B block plane were undoubtedly more effective at promoting the company than at reducing friction between the plane's sole and the wood (see the sidebar on the facing page). The Bailey Tool Company, of Woonsocket, Rhode Island, was founded by Selden Bailey, who originally made his fortune manufacturing clothes-wringing machines. (He was not related to Leonard Bailey, the famous inventor and tool manufacturer who developed the well-known Victor line of handplanes.)

From the collection of John and Janet Wells

Seat-of-the-pants logic will tell you that corrugations on the sole of a handplane should reduce the friction between the plane and the wood. After all, there's less iron touching the surface of the work, right? Unfortunately, testing by modern physical scientists indicates that machined corrugations, holes, or slots into a plane's sole simply do not reduce planing friction and in some cases may actually increase it. However, some sole treatments do help to overcome other shortcomings.

The seven different sole treatments shown in the photo below are on American planes from the Mel Miller Collection. From back to front, they are: (center) Morris' Patent, Knowles type, Steer's Patent; (left) Boston Metallic, Metallic Plane Co.; (right) Rodier's Patent, Holly's Patent. The decorative Morris' Patent (see the photo on pp. 180-181) has distinct diamond-shape corrugations that were designed to prevent hanging up when planing sharp edges or narrow stock, as can happen with straight corrugations. The corrugations

on the bottom of the Knowles-type smooth plane are chevron-shaped, and were cast rather than machined into the bottom of the sole. The c. 1880 Steer's Patent has strips of rosewood securely dovetailed into channels in the iron sole to "prevent the plane from clinging to the work," as an ad claimed. The slotted openings in the sole of the Boston Metallic jack plane were intended not only to lessen friction, but also to reduce the weight of the plane. The straight corrugations on the Metallic Plane Co. Palmer & Storke Patent jack plane are just like those featured on many modern Stanley and Record planes today. But they appeared on Metallic Co. planes nearly 30 years before they became a standard feature on Stanley planes in 1898. The wavy corrugations on the sole of the Rodier's Patent plane (c. 1880) help prevent hang-ups on sharp edges, just as the Morris' Patent plane's sole does. The shallow conical depressions on the c. 1850 Holly's Patent are not cast, but bored during manufacture, using a large drill bit.

Foster's turntable plane

A most unusual mechanism for varying the skew of the blade relative to the work was addressed by the Foster's Patent turntable smoothing plane. Foster, who taught woodworking to children, patented the design in 1907 and produced his turntable planes for only a short time. Probably made by the Ohio Tool company, the Foster's Patent plane was marketed by the Oliver Woodworking Machinery Company. The blade of this plane skewed to more than 45° from square in either direction. This allowed the user to take a cleaner shearing cut while keeping the body of the plane running straight. It also allowed the plane to be used with a shooting board, either right-handed or left-handed.

From the collection of John and Janet Wells

Palmers' plane adjustment mechanism

Known as a Palmers' Metallic Plane at the time of its sale in the 1860s to 1880s, the early-model smoothing, jack, and jointer planes produced by the Auburn, New York, based Metallic Plane Company featured the rather complicated adjustment mechanism shown here. Three levers lock the blade in place and control its lateral alignment and depth of cut. The idea was to allow the user rapid, "one-handed" adjustments.

Mel Miller Collection

Chardoillet's Patent jack-plane adjustment mechanism

Protruding boldly from the top of the plane like the hood ornament of a Phaeton limousine, the elegant cast mechanism atop this Chardoillet's Patent jack plane combines function with beauty. The mechanism was patented in France in about 1852 and adjusts not only the depth of the cutter, but also its pitch. The knob atop the scrolled casting moves the cutter up and down; the thumbscrew at the front of the birch D-handle makes the cutter angle adjustments.

From the collection of John and Janet Wells

THE UNDERTAKER'S BRACE

The pocket-sized cordless drill of its era, this small mid-1900s English folding bit brace (from the collection of Roger K. Smith) was commonly known as an "undertaker's brace." It was the perfect tool for an undertaker or funeral-home director to keep in his suit pocket during services for the deceased. At the conclusion of the viewing of the body, he would take out the compact brace and use a flat-slot bit to drive the screws that secured the lid of the coffin or casket. The brace's upper section swivels, allowing a quick conversion: A thumbscrew is loosened, and the top arm and grip swing around into alignment with the lower arm and chuck. Compact braces were popular among woodworkers as well as undertakers. Around the turn of the century a number of different folding or collapsing mechanisms were patented in America, such as C. W. Stites' folding bit brace (1905) and George Heard's knock-down bit stock, registered in 1906.

Adjustable auger bits

Many designs have been developed that allow the user to bore holes of various diameters with the same bit, including these four patented examples. In the foreground, (right to left): an L. H. Gibbs 1855 patent bit, a lever-adjusted George Hill's Patent expansion bit from 1885, and a William Parmelee's Patent 1874 bit with an arc-shaped cutter. The brace, made by the Hoyt Manufacturing Co. holds a James Swann Patented bit from 1883, which added a spiral twist above the adjustable auger.

Courtesy of Jon Zimmers

Angle-drilling braces and devices

One problem that many a woodworker has had to deal with is boring a hole in a cramped corner or working around an obstruction of some kind. These three braces and two brace attachments are just a few of the multitude of patented devices developed for angled drilling in the late 19th and early 20th centuries. At far right in the photo is the complex-looking two-speed Challenge brace (Morrison Patent, 1898). To change speeds, you remove and refit the chuck from one gear-driven spindle to the other. Below and to the left of the Challenge is a bevel-geared variable angle attachment patented in 1896 by C.A. Meistner that chucks in a regular brace. Just to its left is a Derlon Patent universal jointed brace from 1892 with a cast-iron frame supporting its components. Above the Derlon is a take-down corner brace patented in 1907 by Haberli & Schmidt. For non-angled boring, the tool's long extra handle can be removed and the chuck latched into the remaining brace. Finally, in the upper left corner is a Millers Falls universal-joint-drive adjustable angle drilling attachment, patented in 1880.

From the collection of Don Rosebrook

Fuller's Patent level and inclinometer

The Fuller's Patent level and inclinometer, manufactured
in Pittsburg, Kansas, in the late 1800s, is based on a
mechanism known for thousands of years: the plumb bob.
A pivoting brass enclosure houses a small brass weight
and pointer assembly that indicates plumb. Pivoting the
enclosure to an angle between 0° and 180° allows the
plumb bob to function as an inclinometer.

From the collection of Don Rosebrook

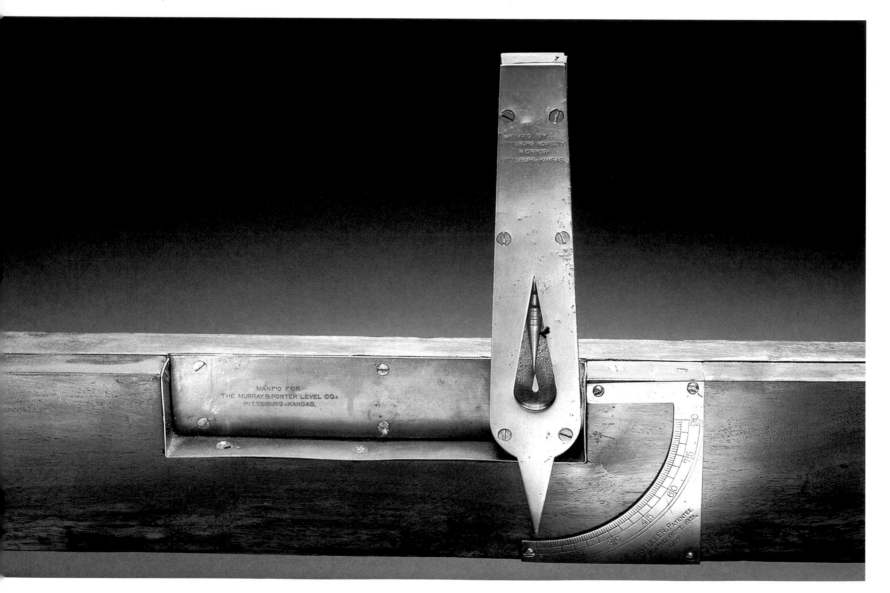

Six inclinometers

Commonly used in construction and railroad work, these six inclinometers cover the range of variations in design these tools have seen in the last 100 years. At top, the Texas Clinometer Company tool, patented in 1908, has a cylinder with a weighted pointer and a scale on the upper edge of an arced metal top. Next down is the Bernard Kern Jr. level, patented in 1906. It has a bubble level attached to a spindle in the center that you can adjust with a scale on the outer edge of the dial. Third down: a No. 3 Frambes from 1884, with a locking pendulum and scale, and a fixed pointer on the outer edge of the dial that is protected by a beveled glass crystal. Fourth from the top is a decoratively bezeled W. B. Melick level, patented in 1889. Like the Frambes, it locks to set the inclinometer angle. The fifth down is a 1921 Loeschner Patent level, which features four bubble vials in addition to a pendulum cursor that reads against a compass printed on oiled paper. At bottom is a Scoville, New York, Patent level from 1859, produced by the J. Terry Company in Rochester, with a spirit-filled rectangular glass vessel, behind which is a protractor scale. After flipping the brass cover plate out of the way, you line up the surface of the liquid with the scale to read the angle.

From the collection of Don Rosebrook

Butler-Taylor inclinometer on Eagle folding adjustable square

A novel means for using a steel rule or square for checking level or angle of incline, the Butler-Taylor inclinometer was a handy little gadget for carpenters to keep in their toolboxes. With a pivoting pointer in the center of a 1½-in.-dia. dial, the device would quickly read any angle between level and plumb. A small bubble vial attached to the pointer assembly allowed the user to zero the device on the tool it was attached to. Here, the Butler-Taylor is clipped to an Eagle 24-in. framing square, the short leg of which can be unlocked and folded in line with the longer leg for transport or storage.

Courtesy of Jon Zimmers

C. Bede level with electric light

Ever try to level ceiling joists in a dark attic? C. Bede was seeking a better way to see the bubble in a level vial when working in a dark work space when he invented and patented his battery-powered, lighted level. Pushing a Bakelite button on the side of the level lights a small bulb that illuminates the level's four vials. The unit's dry-cell battery sits in a compartment behind the name plate.

Courtesy of Jon Zimmers

Direct-reading tape measures

There are lots of different ways that manufacturers of pocket tape measures sought to solve a basic problem faced by all carpenters and cabinetmakers: taking an inside measurement. The four tapes shown here (and discussed front to back) all incorporate some sort of "direct-reading" feature. In the foreground is the X686, made by the Lufkin Rule Co. of Saginaw, Michigan. This tool has a special short tape that's pulled out of the rear of the case. Inside measurements read from a separate scale on the extended steel tape. A couple of small tabs on the bottom of the round case make the tape stand up when laid on a flat surface. The black-cased X1266 was Stanley's first attempt to compete with Lufkin, but it had a much more complicated flip-around-tape mechanism that was fussy to set up. A much more popular tape was the Art Deco styled Stanley Direct Read 6386, with an opening in the case and a pointer for inside measurements. The Master Rule Company's Streamline No. 406 tape was flipped upside-down for inside measurements; dimensions were read through an opening in the case. To make its use easier, the 406 incorporated a small locking lever.

Allan Foster Collection

153

Coping saw with swivel mechanism

Patented in April, 1884, this deep-throated coping saw has an unusual chain mechanism that rotates both blade clamps along with the handle. This feature allows the user to change the angle of the blade while sawing a curved part or complicated fretwork pattern without having to loosen the blade — a real time-saver. The saw, which sports a 12½-in.-long blade, was manufactured and sold by the T. G. Conway Co. of New York.

Courtesy of Jon Zimmers

Carroll Thomas combination tool

This unusual combination tool was patented in 1882 by Carroll Thomas of Lincoln, Illinois, and manufactured by an unknown American maker. The tool combines a basic try square with a bevel gauge, level, marking gauge, butt gauge and even a small rabbet plane. The little lever on the side of the 6-in.-long bronze body locks and releases the diminutive plane's $^{13}/_{16}$-in.-wide blade.

Courtesy of Jon Zimmers

Gladwin's Patent combination tool

One of the more elaborate combination tools to have been manufactured, the Gladwin's Patent combination tool had a small handplane in its handle. At the front of the tool's rosewood body was a simple chuck that accepted the accessories that came with the tool, including a small saw, gimlet, screwdriver, awl, gouge, and chisel. A single knurled thumbscrew locked the tool in the chuck.

From the collection of Bill Phillips

Stanley Odd Job No. 1 multi-tool

The birdhouse shape of Stanley's No. 1 multi-tool, commonly known as the Odd Job, may have lead to many bird-brain jokes in the early part of this century when it was made, but it was a popular tool nonetheless. The Odd Job functioned as a try or miter square. The tool featured a removable scribe and could be used as a marking gauge, center-marking tool, or circle-marking protractor. Level and plumb could be checked with the small vial just below the hole in the center of the tool's body.

Courtesy of Jon Zimmers

Combination hammer/plane

A hammer and a handplane seem an odd couple to combine in a single tool. But paired they are in this hammer/plane made by an unknown manufacturer. What might it have been used for? Examples exist where a small plane was combined with a shingling hatchet; the plane would be used occasionally to trim the edges of shingles to a proper fit. It is quite likely this hammer was also designed for trimming and nailing shingles, although grasping the tool when using the pint-sized plane takes a little getting used to.

From the collection of Bud Steere

Versatile hammer tools

These two household hammers are handy to have around, as they combine several tools into one. The tool at the rear, known as the Household Favorite, is a combination hammer, small hatchet, nail puller, screwdriver (at the head of the hammer end), and wrench. It even has fingers for prying off lids. The tool in the foreground features a tack hammer, candy hammer, and tack puller, with a more substantial cast handle. The hammers are lying on a writing desk whose top is embellished with inlaid decorations. One is particularly interesting: The folding ruler at rear right is a real Stanley boxwood and brass folding rule.

Collection of Roger K. Smith

Johnson Patent hammer/screwdriver

Want to drive screws with the same tool you use to pound nails? If you do, try this J. E. Johnson combination tool (three sizes of which are shown here). The head swivels on the screwdriver shaft for nailing; screws can be driven with the handle in the T position for more leverage. Johnson patented the idea in 1917, but as with many odd combination tools, the concept never really caught on.

From the collection of Dan Comerford

Disston handsaw with Evan's Patent inclinometer

An early crosscut saw marked as a Henry Disston, c. 1858, came with an Evan's patent inclinometer inlaid into its handle. Its blade was also graduated, making it a useful 24-in. rule. The small bead in the notch atop the handle is a little pull-out screwdriver, used for setting the angle of the inclinometer (its straight-slot setscrew is on the other side of the handle). To use the inclinometer, the steel plate bolted to the blade end of the handle was set on the edge of the beam or plank that was being checked for level, or whatever angle the inclinometer was set to.

David Kretchun collection

Combination saw and Archimedean drill

This most unusual tool, signed "Frace-Mobie, 1864," combines a small frame saw with an Archimedean drill. The tool is likely to have belonged to a French casemaker, a highly specialized craftsman who made custom-fitted presentation cases for special objects, such as silverware, jewelry, or dueling pistols. The cases, usually made from secondary woods such as poplar, typically had lots of small dividers and compartments with fussy joinery and small hardware that this combination tool must have been handy for. The end of the handle unscrews for storage of fine drill bits.

From the collection of Wm. R. Robertson

Geometric combination handsaw

Just in case you leave your measuring and layout tools at home, this tool, made by the Geometric Saw Co., combines a 24-in. rule, bevel gauge, and bubble vials for checking plumb and level with a standard crosscut saw. The Geometric's handle is made of Bakelite, one of the earliest synthetic plastics.

From the collection of Don Rosebrook

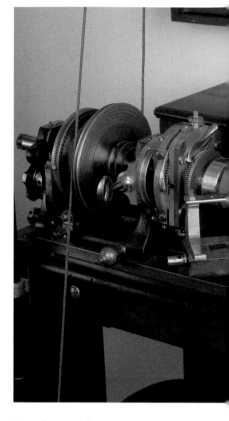

In perfect working condition, Holtzapffel ornamental lathes like the one at left, which was built in about 1880, are helping a whole new generation of woodworkers to create marvelous decorative turnings. A foot treadle powers not only the rotation of the lathe itself, but also an overhead system that drives special cutters used for decorative work. The tools in the wall cabinet all have different edge profiles and are used for freehand ornamental turning work.

The complex-looking headstock is at the heart of the Holtzapffel lathe. It allows the work to be turned as on a regular lathe and also indexed by means of its brass indexing plate (to the left, with all the holes in it). With the work locked at various positions, patterns can be cut into its surface with cutters mounted on the lathe's slide rest. The cutters are driven by thin belts powered by a shaft above the lathe bed, dentist-drill style.

P rior to the development of the ornamental turning lathe, if wood turners wanted to add decoration to a piece, they had to do it by hand-carving the turning after it came off the lathe. Ornamental turning, the art of decoratively machining a lathe-mounted turning, had been in practice for several centuries when toolmaker John Jacob Holtzapffel left Strasbourg, Alsace, for London, were he opened a lathe-making business in 1794. The important innovation that Holtzapffel developed for his excellent-quality foot-powered lathes was the overhead drive system. A treadle-driven flywheel was coupled by a system of pulleys and flexible-cord drive belts (like an old-fashioned dentist's drill) to power a revolving cutter. The motion of the cutting tool was controlled by a slide rest (like the rest on a machinist's lathe). By fitting any of a wide variety of cutters, the user could create an unending profusion of surface decorations on a turning blank while it was mounted on the lathe. Further shaping and decorating could be executed by employing a myriad of lathe accessories, such as indexing heads, special chucks, cutting frames, and spiral or curvilinear geared apparatuses.

As Holtzapffel's reputation as a first-class lathe maker grew, his lathes achieved great popularity with wealthy amateur woodworkers, as well as with English and European royalty. His customers included Archduke Otto Von Hapsburg of Austria, Wilhelm III, King of the Netherlands, and even Queen Victoria of England.

After building more than 2,500 ornamental lathes, the Holtzapffel company closed its doors in 1928. The lathe shown at left, which was built c. 1880, is from the collection of Steve Johnson.

Holtzapffel geared chuck

Countless accessory devices may be mounted on a Holtzapffel lathe to create a nearly infinite variety of ornamental forms and decorative applications. This complex geared chuck was used to create complex spiral patterns, the size and shape of which depend on the combination of gears chosen. Most original Holtzapffel accessories originally came in beautifully fitted boxes, as did this set.

From the collection of Fred Armbruster

Holtzapffel rose engine

Of all the Holtzapffel lathes that were built, the rose engine was among the most unusual in design. This highly specialized lathe is able to move the work through a complex orbit, the shape of which is determined by the user by the choice of a shaped cam called a rosette (as shown in the center of the headstock area in the photo below). Riding against stationary followers, the headstock not only rotates, but also pivots back and forth according to the shape of the rosette being used. Rosettes can be elliptical, square, or multi-sided, or they can have more elaborate profiles. Some have lobes like the petals of a flower, which is how this model got its name.

Since extremely few rose-engine ornamental lathes exist today (and those that do rarely come to auction), ornamental turner Fred Armbruster decided to build his own. Starting with measurements he took off a vintage rose-engine lathe at London's Science Museum, Armbruster built two reproductions from scratch, manufacturing most of the parts himself. He completed the project in six years and sold one of the lathes to defray the cost of the project.

From the collection of Fred Armbruster

Ornamental turnings

The forte of the Holtzapffel ornamental turning lathe is its ability to cut an unlimited number of different shapes and decorations on either the outside or inside of a turning. These two vessels, made by English turners Paul Fletcher and Michael Brooks, are shown on the bed of a standard Holtzapffel lathe that's fitted with an eccentric chuck. The small box in front, by Fletcher, is made of African blackwood with a brass and white celluloid band around its midsection. The lid is inlaid with an ivory ring and pink ivory wood insert. The designs incised on the lid were done on a rose-engine lathe (see the photo at right on the facing page). The tall vessel at right, by Brooks, is made from ebony and has spiral decorations on its body and a tapered spiral finial—classic touches in the practice of ornamental turning.

From the collection of Steve Johnson

TOOLS WITH THE
DECORATIVE TOUCH

While function dictates that basic tools need not look fancy to work well, both makers and users often choose to embellish their tools. Decoration adds an extra dimension that makes an otherwise simple tool special. And although adornment won't make a tool more precise or help it function more efficiently, it has other benefits. A finely wrought tool can help to weave inspiration into the fabric of daily labor and make onerous tasks easier and more pleasurable.

In earlier eras, people seem to have had more time to decorate the implements of their daily lives. The surviving examples from Europe, Asia, and the Americas offer proof that such decoration is an ancient custom. Why did early craftsmen go to the trouble of decorating their tools? One of the prime motivations undoubtedly

was religion. Many early European tools are adorned with Christian motifs, including incised crucifixes and sacred initials. Decoration in the form of a carved monogram or an inlaid family crest could also serve to personalize a tool and mark it as one's own; such a tool might become an heirloom to be passed on with great pride (this is still common practice today). In some cases, craftsmen lavishly decorated their tools to impress their colleagues and improve their social status.

Most decorative tools started life as plain tools that later had modest amounts of ornamentation added to them. On old wood-bodied planes, such decoration often took the form of chip-carved or painted initials, floral designs, or inlaid patterns or marquetry. Sometimes metal punches were used to create a repeating pattern, such as a simple rope border around the sole of the plane or a more complex floral pattern to cover the side of the body. Early metal-bodied planes were occasionally painted, etched, or decoratively engraved.

With the passage of time, the meaning of many of the old decorative motifs has been lost, and today one can only speculate on their original significance. For example, the punch marks and chasing found on early forged axes and plane blades may have served as the signature of the maker or an indication of where the tool was made. In other cases, they were added simply for decoration.

Some tools received more embellishment in the form of carved or painted animals, people, even religious scenes. These ornate decorations bear witness to the woodworker's love for nature, family, country, and spirituality. Carving in low relief was commonly applied to wood-bodied planes, as was the inlaying of multicolored woods and bone and ivory. The fanciest tools were artistically rendered and carved in the round.

Although it is logical to assume that decorated tools were few and far between when compared to plain "working" tools,

enough fancy planes have survived from 17th- and 18th-century Europe to make it clear that decorative "user" tools were more the rule than the exception. In that time period, the Dutch produced lines of "standard" bench planes that include the date (year) as a significant part of their decoration. These "mass-produced" planes were in fact made by hand, and each is a unique object that bears witness to the whims and talents of the maker—an extra whorl here, a chip-carved scroll there.

Fortunately, the practice of decorating woodworking tools didn't die out with the coming of the Machine Age. Quite the opposite occurred: Mass-produced metal tools of the late 19th and early 20th centuries were often highly decorated, with stylish Victorian embellishments cast or machined into the iron bodies and handles of hand tools. Some of the high points from this era are the Morris'

Patent planes, one of which is shown on pp. 180-181. Such lavish ornamentation may perhaps have had an ulterior motive: increasing the perceived value of these tools and enhancing their sales appeal.

Hand tools weren't the only woodworking implements that were embellished. The frames and stands of machines were often shapely and commonly bore decorative elements. For example, the cast-iron base of a lathe or scrollsaw might rest on delicate feet that resemble talons or lion's paws. Machines were often finished with colorful paint jobs, and their frames outlined with contrasting stripes.

The tools in this chapter have been selected to take the reader on a colorful tour of the many different ways that tools have been decorated in the past. The earliest examples are European wooden tools that have been crafted and adorned by their users. As you feast your eyes on the carving, also take note of the rich patina—a lovely sort of decoration in its own right. Decorative tools made in the 19th and 20th centuries are in the next part, including

some finely cast metal tools that display the Victorian predilection for elaborate design. The chapter concludes with a few contemporary decorated tools, many of which are common tools straight from the hardware store or flea market that were embellished by the owner. Perhaps they will inspire you to add a few special touches to the tools you have in your shop right now.

One more thing. Elaborately decorated woodworking tools aren't limited to this chapter; they appear throughout the book. After reading this chapter, you may want to revisit the other chapters, this time focusing on the tools' decorative aspects. You will be rewarded with a deeper appreciation for the level of craftsmanship and additional insight into the significance of the tools. ▨

Dolphin and dragon planes

Both of the remarkable tools shown above are early
European handplanes. The plane on the right has a carved
horn that is reminiscent of the prow of a Viking ship,
suggesting that the tool may have been of Scandinavian
origin and used in shipbuilding. The 14-in.-long plane's
"dragon" horn (detail, right) is carved from boxwood, while its
body is hornbeam. Possibly to repair excess wear, the bottom
of the plane has an overlay of thin sheet brass, bent in place
and nailed around the edges with small handmade pins.
The remarkable plane on the left is known as the
Anstruther plane, a name that comes from its years of display
at the Fisheries Museum in Anstruther, Scotland. The
19-in.-long fore plane is made of fruitwood and was
likely once used by an early Glaswegian boatbuilder.
The Anstruther plane's horn is carved in the form
of a mythical dolphin, providing a comfortable
grip (see the photo at left on p. 224). Atop the body
is a relief-carved portrait of an Elizabethan
gentleman (detail, left). The plane has a simple
blade-adjusting mechanism with a single
large screw that engages a slot in the iron.
The plane's mouth has a whalebone insert in
the shape of Cupid's bow to narrow the opening,
probably compensating for wear.

From the collection of Roger B. Phillips

EVERY PATINA TELLS A STORY

Part of the beauty of early wooden tools is the remarkable patina that develops on them from years of use. The patina is the surface gloss that shows the signs of aging on the wood. The aging of a traditional varnish or oil finish, such as linseed oil, can make a rather ordinary blond wood, such as beech or maple, look darker and richer. Years of handling, wear, and exposure to dust and sunlight also contribute to the warm glow that old wooden tools usually have. This patina is almost always uneven, showing where a tool received the most wear and indicating how it was held. In some cases, a tight grip is evidenced by depressions worn into the wood, such as on the sides or top of a handplane. Such markings serve as a graphic depiction of how the tool was used, as well as providing intriguing clues to the character of the tool's owners.

Tyrolean jointer plane

This 17th-century Tyrolean carved fruitwood jointer plane bears an artistically rendered acanthus-leaf carving that extends down into the throat area. The plane lacks any sort of rear handle; an iron nail just behind the cutter originally secured a leather strap that served as a hand loop. The user grasped the body of the plane during cutting and used the leather loop to help pull back the long, heavy plane after each stroke.

From the collection of John and Janet Wells

German miter plane

This early German miter plane is unusual in construction with an iron sole nearly ¼ in. thick that's banded to a wood body with a heavy iron strap that runs across the midsection of the plane. The strap also provides a means of securing the wedge and iron assembly to the body. Front and rear, pairs of large iron screws secure the ends of the sole to the body. The plane's most notable feature, though, is the carved mouth area, with its grotesque face, flowing beard, and piercing eyes. The shape of the head is like a violin, perhaps indicating that the user was an instrument maker.

From the collection of Roger B. Phillips

Moisset plane

Known as the Moisset plane for the name of the French collection of which it was once a part, this charming tool packs a lot of personality into its 4-in. length. Every surface of the plane is decorated—even the sole has a narrow band of chip carving! Made of boxwood that has acquired a deep color and rich patina, this small smoothing plane has an obscure working history. It shows signs of prolonged wear (the mouth has been repaired with a small arrow-shaped ebony inlay), yet the wedge seems never to have been made fully functional. A male face with a star on its forehead is carved into the plane's horn; in its mouth it holds a cryptic symbol: a drooping two-headed arrow. Arrows also pierce the heart carved at the rear of the plane (detail, below).

From the collection of Roger B. Phillips

Harrison miter plane

Purchased by its current owner at an English auction, this early Harrison miter plane has a masterfully carved rosewood front grip in the form of a Scottish gentleman wearing a traditional tam-o'-shanter. It was not uncommon in the 19th-century British Isles for craftsmen to buy the metal body and cutter of a plane and make the wood infills themselves.

From the collection of Valdis Petersons

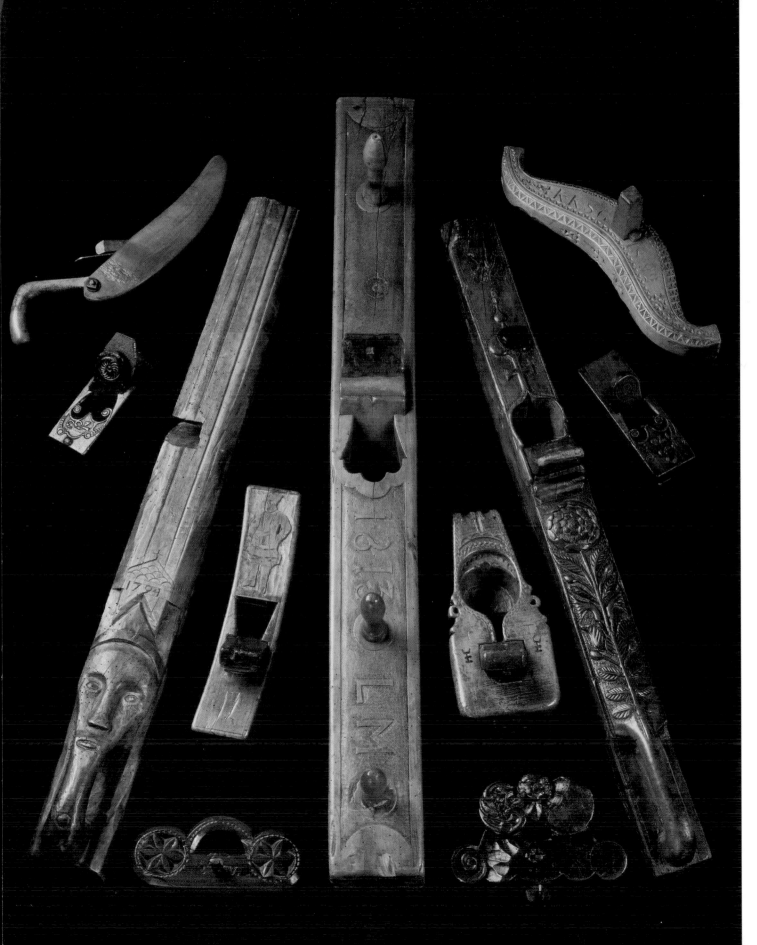

European handplanes

These 18th- and 19th-century planes, from the Arthur Pascal collection, are embellished with symbols, figures of men and natural objects, and simple decorative chip carving. (Note that the router plane at the bottom, just right of center, was originally only half finished; only the left side has been fully carved.) In 1991, Pascal donated the collection to the Canadian Museum of Civilization in Ottawa, Ontario, where the tools now are kept.

DUTCH STANDARD HANDPLANES

lthough most late 17th- and early 18th-century handplanes in Europe were made by tradesmen for their own use, there was a distinct plane-making industry in the Netherlands. Working in small family workshops, Dutch craftsmen produced lines of wood handplanes that were made to a standard template and sold over the counter to tradesmen. Typically, these planes were adorned with decorations including whorls and scrolls carved into both the body and the wedge. Most of these planes bear the date of their manufacture. Although these planes were made to a standard, each was a unique, hand-made object with slight variations in decoration.

The Dutch standard handplanes shown in the photo below are from the collection of Roger B. Phillips. Dated between 1730 and 1795, they illustrate the variations that were common to these planes. The small plane in the center of the photo is a scroll-shaped scrub plane *(gerfshaaf)*. The plane at front left is a *blokschaaf* smoothing plane. This plane has a nicely carved front grip, and the wedge has a lady's face carved into it. At front right is a *roffel* jack plane dated 1774, which has a convex sole for hollowing. In the back row are three *bossingschaafen,* which are planes used for panel raising. Each has a skewed iron for cleaner cuts in woods with figured grain. The plane at rear center, marked 1791, and the plane at rear left, dated 1730, once had a dark stain applied over the blond beechwood. Iron buttons atop most of these plane bodies are for tapping with a small hammer, which is necessary when adjusting the iron on a wood plane.

European cooper's plane

Dated 1802, this European cooper's plane has chip-carved decorations
including a spiral whorl and a six-petal flower atop the body. The
individual pips carved in rows along the sides alternate directions and
may have offered the user a better grip. The top of the 3-ft.-long birch
body at both the front and rear has extra sets of holes for legs that
would allow the plane to be used in an inverted position for jointing
long barrel staves. In the tray of the tool chest are three Dutch planes,
which also are decorated with traditional chip-carved patterns.

From the collection of Clifford R. Sapienza

European plane with herringbone trim

Probably adorned by its user, the entire rim of both fore and aft infills of this cast-iron plane body is decorated with alternating parallelograms of "rope" inlay. The handle, fore grip, and body are made of Brazilian rosewood with ebony and pearwood banding. Like many early metal-bodied planes, this plane has an attractive cast-bronze lever cap that's massive enough to do a good job of damping any cutter vibration that might occur while planing.

From the collection of John and Janet Wells

Shoulder rabbet plane with marquetry

Starting with what was probably a commercially made iron and rosewood shoulder plane, the proud owner added a personal touch by inlaying his initials as part of a decorative floral pattern. The entire bouquet and surrounding border were cut from a single piece of mahogany veneer and mortised into the plane's rosewood infill.

From the collection of Clifford R. Sapienza

Inlaid level and inclinometer

While many tool owners identify their tools by stamping in their initials, there are much more decorative possibilities. The mahogany body of this user-made level and inclinometer, patterned after a tool patented by Magnus Nilson, has been inlaid with a fancy monogram executed in marquetry.

From the collection of Don Rosebrook

Two carved braces

These braces, of unknown origin, have the kind of fanciful carving that often adorned early user-made tools. On the brace at far left, the bit pad is threaded into the chuck. The bit end of this brace was burned in a fire and has been restored. The other brace was found in central Florida, but its carving suggests early African-American folk art. The head of this brace is the carved face of a man; the large open mouth shows the wedged end of the shaft that secures the brace's rotating head (detail, above). The iron-banded wooden chuck and early spiral bit suggest that this brace was made in the mid-19th century.

Collection of Ronald W. Pearson, D.O.

French brace with man's portrait

The maker of this early French brace found an unusual way of keeping a photograph of a family hero or famous person close at hand: by implanting a small printed image into the head of the tool. The picture of the mustachioed, monocle-wearing man (likely a military officer) is set beneath an isinglass (mica) window, framed by concentric rings of brass escutcheon pins.

Collection of Eric M. Peterson

Brace and bow drill

This handsome brace and bow drill have the look and feel of vintage tools, but both were made in 1978 by Waverly, Nebraska, woodworker Titus Johnson. The body of the brace, right, is tiger maple, stained dark, while the bow drill, far right, is fashioned from rosewood with brass ferrules. Both tools are signed and dated and have ivory inlays with a scrimshawed design of a fly, which is Johnson's hallmark.

Collection of Eric M. Peterson

Plane with floral carving

Although this 10-in.-long beechwood plane is many years old, the floral carving was done in recent years by Seattle-area tool collector Al Anderson. Imitating the style of relief carving often found on vintage European planes, Anderson transformed a plain tool into an attractive piece. To lend the carving more visual depth, he used a chasing tool to impress a pebbly texture onto the background.

From the collection of Steven F. Dice

Ebony block and shoulder planes

Made of Macassar ebony, these small planes by Curtis Bowden show great simplicity in design. Made for his own use, the block plane (left) and shoulder plane (right) both bear Bowden's monogram, inlaid in silver. The block plane's frog and iron are engraved, adding ornament to the simple form. The iron on the shoulder plane is skewed to yield cleaner cuts on highly figured hardwoods.

From the collection of Curtis Bowden

Engraved metal planes

Curtis Bowden doesn't have a cabinet full of rare or exotic handplanes in his shop, but through his own efforts, he has no shortage of unique and beautiful tools. Bowden has transformed several stock Stanley handplanes, including the No. 27 block plane shown at right and the Bedrock jack plane shown below, from common to extraordinary by adorning them with decorations he engraved on the plain sides of the iron-bodied planes.

From the collection of Curtis Bowden

178

The engraved designs Curtis Bowden creates are original, though the motifs are common to the engravings found on expensive firearms. Here, Bowden carefully works his signature into the floral pattern he engraved into the side of the Bedrock jack plane shown below and at bottom on the facing page.

Using original floral designs composed of motifs that are common to gun engravings, woodworker and toolmaker Curtis Bowden has developed a unique way to embellish his collection of standard handplanes. Bowden employs traditional engraving practices that are performed using special tools called burins. The burins (many of which Bowden made himself) have sharp points in a variety of shapes—square, half-round, diamond, and so on. The point is pushed over the metal surface, forming grooves and cross-hatching that are used to create designs. During the process, the plane is held rock steady in a special engraver's vise (see the photo at left). Bowden says that cast iron is actually fairly easy to engrave compared to softer metals such as silver and brass, which require more refined tool control to engrave cleanly.

Early on, Bowden learned the secret to success. "The trick is to give a design depth and dimension, even though it is only a scant $\frac{1}{16}$ in. deep in actual relief," he says. For example, the illusion of depth in the engraved designs shown in the work on these pages is achieved by making the pattern of leaves and vines overlap. Cross-hatched lines indicate shading where elements cross. Embossing the background with chasing tools darkens it and gives the design more depth.

After engraving is complete, Bowden buffs the finished surfaces. He allows the polishing compound to remain in the crevices to help make the designs stand out.

Morris' Patent iron jointer plane

One of the most distinctive of all production planes, the Morris' Patent iron jointer plane shown at right has a lovely floral design cast into the upper surface of the sole. Although the elaborate casting didn't affect the performance, it certainly bolstered the pride of its owner. The beech-handled planes, available in smooth and jack-plane models as well, were patented in 1870 and manufactured by the Sandusky Tool Company. The soles of the Morris' Patent planes were as distinctive as the tops, with a cast diamond pattern (see the sidebar on p. 145).

From the collection of John and Janet Wells

Cast-iron inclinometer

Fancy cast-iron work was not uncommon on better-quality tools manufactured in the late 19th century—especially plow planes and levels. Unfortunately, such delicate work was also quite fragile, and many tools that were "daily users" survive only in broken condition. The manufacturer of this level and inclinometer is unknown; the maker's paper labels probably fell off years ago.

From the collection of George Gaspari

Victorian plane

This 2nd Model No. 42 Miller's Patent plane is lavished with extensive Victorian ornamentation, from its gunmetal frame to its twin fences and filletster bottom.

Mel Miller Collection

Compass-plane knobs

For both users and collectors, details add a lot of appeal to many otherwise plain tools. These fancy nickel-plated knobs show a couple of the decorative variations found on several planes made by Bailey and Stanley, in this case two compass planes: a Stanley No. 113 (in the foreground) and a Bailey Victor No. 20. The latter is also shown in the top photo on p. 59.

Mel Miller Collection

Stanley No. 110 lever caps

The Stanley No. 110 block plane, said to be the most popular of the non-adjustable block planes, had a most decorative lever cap (on the plane at far right) when it was first produced in 1876. Unfortunately, the ornate belt-buckle-like cap was probably too delicate, and was quickly changed to the more conventional lever cap on the plane at right, with but a simple six-point star adorning the top of the casting.

Courtesy of Jon Zimmers

Advertising tape measures

In the early 20th century, advertising tape measures were made by the hundreds by various companies to hawk everything from elevators and asphalt to tools, lumber, and coffins. Such tapes were usually given away to customers, a practice that continues today. In this assortment, note the dramatic, deeply embossed pattern on the Otis Elevator company tape; the brass-cased Stanley advertising tape; and the celluloid-case tape with the lady's face by William McNeese, a Philadelphia toolmaking company that specialized in saws and bevels.

Allan Foster Collection

Knowles iron jointer plane

One of the more elaborately
painted production handplanes
was the Knowles iron jointer
plane. The body of the plane
was painted brown to set off the
gold and red pinstriping and
decorative shields. This Knowles
plane, from the Oliver Deming
collection, was probably
produced in the mid-1800s. It is
topped off with a beech handle,
wedge, and front knob.

Courtesy Roger K. Smith, Patented
Transitional & Metallic Planes In
America, Vol II; *(photo by Joseph Szaszfai)*

Morris' Patent scissors-type plow plane

The floral decoration on this c. 1871 Morris' Patent iron plow plane, from the John Harkness collection, is original, but it isn't painted on. It is actually an applied decal (most existing examples of this plane have only traces of the decal left). The scissors-type adjustable fence is unique to plow planes. Loosening two thumbscrews adjusts the fence for plowing dadoes or grooves up to 10 in. from the edge of the work.

Courtesy Roger K. Smith, Patented Transitional & Metallic Planes In America, Vol II; (photo by Joseph Szaszfai)

Harmon sight level

Patented in 1880, this builder's transit was made by
John W. Harmon of Boston, Massachusetts. Meant to be
mounted on a wooden tripod, the transit has a nickel-
plated top tube that has no optics, only a peep sight and
crosshairs that a builder used to sight markers in the
process of laying out a foundation or a wall. As was
typical of late 19th-century manufactured tools, the transit
was painted brightly to make it more attractive and to
justify its relatively high purchase price.

From the collection of Don Rosebrook

Painted cast-iron level

Paint jobs as elaborate as the gold and green paint on this Nicholson's Patent cast-iron level were not uncommon on tools made in the late 19th century.

From the collection of Patrick and Lisa Leach

With its original black paint and gold and red pinstriping intact, this Barnes No. 6 scrollsaw is a collector's dream. This velocipede-style saw, which has fixed cast-iron arms supporting a spring-loaded reciprocating blade assembly, was pedaled by the seated user. Round leather belts transmit power from the large lower flywheel to run the saw, as well as a small drill. The saw's belts have been replaced, as has the round wooden saw table.

Amazing as it may seem, much of the equipment that now forms a basic complement of electrically powered machines in the modern woodshop was once powered by the craftsman's own feet. In the 19th and early 20th centuries, foot power was applied to all manner of early machine tools, including scrollsaws, lathes, drill presses, spindle shapers (then known as molders or formers), and even table saws.

Two methods of transferring power from the human foot to the whirring tool predominated: treadles and pedals. Treadle power was the system used on the Seneca Falls Empire scrollsaw and drill at left. (Treadles are still seen in at least one device in common use—the treadle-powered sewing machine.) Pedal power, which was sometimes known as velocipede power after early bicycle propulsion, was used on the Barnes No. 6 scrollsaw and drill shown on the facing page. Both machines are from the collection of Steve Johnson.

Treadles and pedals create rotary motion, which was transferred to the machine's arbor, spindle, or other mechanism by means of leather belts wrapped around cast-iron pulleys. Many machines had a large iron flywheel that stored energy to help the tool's blade or bit spin around at a more consistent rate of speed. A flywheel mechanism was a boon to the user, who wouldn't have to pump furiously the whole time the machine was being used—the flywheel's stored energy could keep it going for a short time.

The most eye-catching feature of foot-powered tools is their cast-iron frames. These often had components that were sculptural, such as decorative feet and tractor-like seats. And like so many other cast-iron tools of the time, the frames of foot-powered machines often bore colorful hand-painted pinstriping, decorative patterns, trade names, and other designs.

Sporting a beautiful paint job and extensive pinstriping, the Seneca Falls Empire scroll-saw has an additional arm mounted to the side of its cast-iron frame that supports a small drill press. This feature allowed the user to bore small holes in stock to pass the thin blade through to start an inside cut. This was useful for the pierced fretwork commonly done in Victorian times. A ring atop the drill arm acts as a handle to engage or disengage the drill press.

MINIATURE 8 MARVELS

It is within our nature as human beings to take pleasure in small things. Babies, toddlers, puppies, and kittens are universally adored, leaving even the most serious adults cooing and babbling in a laughable high-pitched voice. In fact, most things have delightful small-scale counterparts; for the guitar, a ukulele; for the mansion, the cottage. In the woodworking world, there are miniature tools. Whether they were created out of the needs of the craftsman or the whimsy of the modeler, small-scale tools are apt to evoke a smile and a chuckle from even the most practical woodworker.

In the professional woodshop, pint-sized tools are occasionally built out of necessity. Many types of work require small parts to be planed and shaped; the modelmaker, patternmaker, and instrument maker all work wood on such a scale as part of their daily routine. Even a regular cabinetmaker occasionally requires petite tools—bantam-size miter planes and rabbet planes can be mighty handy when shaping parts for a delicate display case or fancy jewelry chest. Tools such as instrument maker's finger planes may look like items straight from Tom Thumb's tool chest, but they are in fact

designed to be manipulated by adult hands—pushed by fingertips or the palm.

Then there is the world of modelmaking and miniature creations that replicate their full-sized counterparts. Scaling down an object such as a ship, car, airplane, or tool presents the engaging challenge of making the replica appear as if it were the actual object shrunken down, with each feature accurate in every detail. There is great delight to be found in closely inspecting a masterfully constructed miniature.

Many well-crafted miniature tools have intricate mechanisms; for example, the fully adjustable blade assembly on a plane that's no bigger than a fingernail. Most of these tiny tools can actually cut wood, but their size makes them better suited to the hands of a Lilliputian woodwright.

Making miniature tools can require extraordinary dexterity and patience. Marking out, cutting, shaping, sanding, and finishing the dozens of minute parts required for the average mini usually take a lot more time than building the tool in full size. Special jigs and fixtures must be made to hold and position parts for machining and assembly. Even the tools used to make miniature replicas often have to be made by the builder. For example, special table saws with small-diameter blades and super-fine teeth are necessary for cutting tiny parts without tearout while maintaining extreme accuracy. The smallest parts (screws, nails, pins, springs) that are used to assemble miniature tools are installed in the same way as they are on their full-size counterparts, but mini fasteners are so small that they must be handled entirely with tweezers. Machining and fabrication

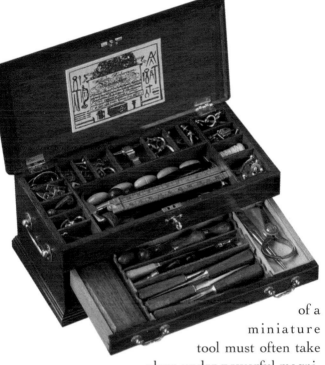

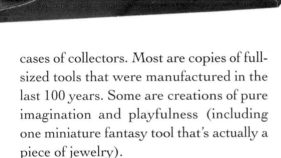

of a miniature tool must often take place under powerful magnification, so the maker must have exceptionally good eyesight. The finest details, such as minuscule increments incised into tiny rules and scales, stamped initials, and engraved designs (see the ivory and silver brace shown on p. 204) demand special tools and techniques, as well as exceptional skill, to execute convincingly.

The challenge of rendering a convincing miniature can also involve the proper choice of materials.

Woods commonly used for full-sized tools, such as oak or beech, have a large grain figure and pores that are too large to look believable when made into smaller objects. For miniature woodworking tools, makers typically employ hardwoods with very dense, tight grain, such as ebony, boxwood, and lignum vitae. Sometimes, miniaturists will make their tools from rare woods, such as snakewood or pink ivory, or special materials, such as horn, ivory, sterling silver, or gold, to make their small-scale creations even more precious and desirable.

This chapter begins with some of the bantam-size tools users have built to earn an honest day's work, including both vintage and modern tools taken from the tool chests of working craftsmen. The second portion of the chapter features miniature tools from the display

cases of collectors. Most are copies of full-sized tools that were manufactured in the last 100 years. Some are creations of pure imagination and playfulness (including one miniature fantasy tool that's actually a piece of jewelry).

When photographing anything that's looks "real" size but in reality is much smaller, the challenge is to convey a sense of scale without resorting to hackneyed practices, such as including a coin or ruler in the shot. Here, I've tried to invent a few fresh visual clues with each tool to give you an immediate sense of how small it actually is. In the detail shots you will be able to see clearly just how delicately crafted many of these tools are. If you are like me, a close examination of these tools will leave you in awe of the high levels of skill and dexterity exercised by the makers of these marvelous little creations. ▨

Palm plane

Sometimes called "violin maker's planes," palm planes are used for shaping the bodies of hollow wooden musical instruments. With its extended handle, this instrument maker's palm plane would be easier to control than a plane that lacks a handle, particularly when working inside the cramped quarters of an assembled violin, viola, or cello.

From the collection of John and Janet Wells

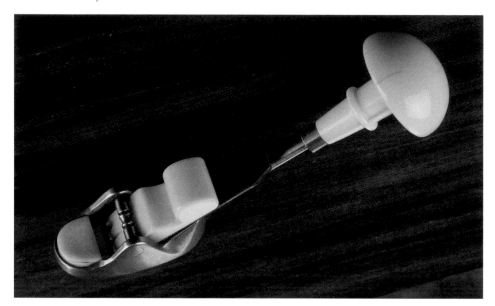

Ivory instrument maker's plane

Believed to have been carved from a whale's tooth, this small instrument maker's plane was found in a seaman's chest on the coast of Maine. The spoon-shaped sole (convex in both directions) is just right for hollowing out the body of a stringed musical instrument. The plane—only slightly longer than 1 in.—has a delicately carved front scroll that some might say resembles a stylized whale's tail. A brass crosspiece holds the ivory wedge and iron in place.

Collection of Frank Kosmerl

Brass plane with bone wedge

With an iron sole dovetailed to its brass body just like larger miter planes, this 2-in.-long plane was clearly designed for finer tasks, such as refining delicate miters or shaving petite parts to size. Engraved with the maker's name, Edwd. J. Davies, and sporting a lovely bone wedge and infill, the plane may have belonged to an instrument maker.

From the collection of John and Janet Wells

Instrument maker's planes

Shaping and smoothing jobs inside the body of a musical instrument, such as a ukulele (shown here), require a wide range of different-sized planes. These instrument maker's planes range in length from 3½ in. down to less than 1 in. Although they are not a matched set, all the planes feature a traditional acanthus leaf at the front, which on the smaller planes serves as a rest for the user's finger and on the larger planes serves as a front grip. All but one of the planes have bodies fabricated from iron and/or brass with rosewood wedges and infills; the plane at far right has an ivory infill and wedge. Most of the planes are fitted with serrated blades, which minimized tearout when taking heavier cuts on woods with squirrely or figured grain.

From the collection of Roger B. Phillips

French engraved plane

With a shape reminiscent of a Turkish slipper, this small French instrument maker's plane has a convex sole for shaping the inside of hollow wooden instruments. The plane, found in an antique shop across from the Louvre, has graceful lines that are nicely accented by the floral engraving on the sides of the brass body.

From the collection of John and Janet Wells

Scottish palm plane

Rather petite in contrast to the full-sized bench planes surrounding it, this Scottish palm plane has an upturned handle that provides an excellent grip and leverage for its user. The plane is handy for trimming and surface cleanup on small casework pieces and for work on musical instruments.

From the collection of John and Janet Wells

Bronze and ebony shoulder plane

Only about 3 in. long, this English pattern shoulder plane has a cast-bronze body with decorative angular ebony infill and matching wedge. It's a handy tool for trimming joints or frame members for small and delicate assemblies, such as jewelry boxes and display cases.

From the collection of Roger B. Phillips

Scale brass and wood rabbet planes

These small-sized rabbet planes were made by Seattle, Washington, machinist, tool maker, and collector Joe Hraska. Based on full-sized English style "rebate" planes, these plane bodies are constructed from brass. Hraska dovetailed the soles on, as was traditionally done (see the photo on p. 38). He then fitted rosewood infills and wedges to the pair of planes, adding a row of ivory dots to the one with the serpentine top for panache.

Courtesy of Darrell Six

Chip-decorated small plane and spokeshave

Extensive chip carving and the style of decoration on these two small tools suggest that they were likely made in Canada or northern Maine. The plane, at rear, is only 5 in. long, with a ¾-in.-wide iron. The spokeshave in front of it shows a lot of wear and bears the name of its owner, Jon Hedogod.

From the collection of Patrick and Lisa Leach

Pint-sized Bailey Victor planes

With their red paint jobs and nickel finish intact, these two small planes are among the most collectible models made by inventor and toolmaker Leonard Bailey. The toy-sized Bailey Little Victor No. 51, at right in the photo, uses a cog wheel and machine screw to secure its 1-in.-wide iron. The Bailey Victor No. 12½, to its left, is only slightly larger than the No. 51. These planes were produced by Bailey after he had a royalties squabble with the Stanley Rule & Level Co., which manufactured many of Bailey's designs.

From the collection of Patrick and Lisa Leach

Chaplin No. 1 handplane

Lots of manufacturers produced diminutive bench planes. The best known is the much sought-after, toy-like Stanley No. 1, but the $5\frac{3}{8}$-in.-long Chaplin No. 1 is rarer and more attractive than its similar-sized Stanley cousin. The Chaplin No. 1 has nickel-plated iron grips and a novel adjustment lever with a threaded section that engages the underside of the iron. Flipping the lever from side to side raises and lowers the blade.

From the collection of George Gaspari

It's hard to believe that this replica of an 18th-century gentleman's tool chest packed with tools is only 2 in. long! A masterful 1/12-scale reproduction by celebrated miniaturist William Robertson, the chest is made of mopane and pearwood, with cast-brass Rococo drop handles and beaded backplates. The minuscule lock actually works, and the label on the underside of the lid is printed on 18th-century paper—in lettering to perfect scale, of course.

The miniature tool chest was made with the same construction as the original. Tool trays and drawers are fully dovetailed with hand-sawn dust boards. The dividers are V-notched and crosslapped. The lid sides are tongue and groove.

Robertson's tool chest contains all the same tools that were found in the original, including a Kent-style hatchet, claw hammer, five gimlets, a jack plane, divider, awl, round file, burnisher, inside/outside calipers, folding rule, bevel gauge, marking gauge, try square, backsaw, three turnscrews, a smooth plane, saw wrest, four brad awls, an oilstone in its case, three tanged chisels, a mallet, a riveting hammer, a beak anvil, two gouges, and shears. All the tools are fully functional, with blades made of steel. Other parts are brass with handles made of pearwood, boxwood, Bolivian rosewood, African blackwood, and maple. The chest and tools took about 1,000 hours to complete.

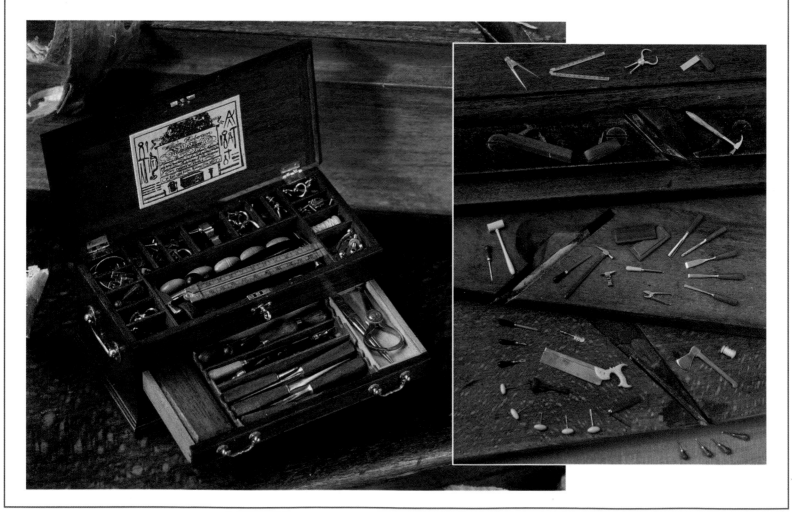

Nuremberg mini-plane

A recreation of one of the remarkable Nuremberg planes made in Germany in the 16th century, this miniature was made by English miniaturist David Brookshaw. Fabricated entirely from iron, the miniature is faithful to the original, except that on the original Nuremberg plane the etching is not nearly as clear as on the miniature, due to corrosion. The 2⅛-in.-long plane is shown alongside an ivory folding rule.

Collection of Ronald W. Pearson, D.O.

French "music" handplane

This scale reproduction of a famous French violin maker's plane dated 1719 brings new life to the expression "whistle while you work." The sides of the iron plane were engraved with a musical ode to the plane written by the maker. The plane's front grip is shaped in the form of a stylized scallop shell. This 2⅞-in.-long reproduction was made by David Brookshaw, who etched the design in the sides of the plane by using an acid resist technique.

From the collection of Roger B. Phillips

Miniature reproductions

The tiny planes shown above were all made by miniaturist David
Brookshaw. At right is a ⅓-scale miniature of the well-known Cupid
plane, an original boxwood plane thought to be of French origin
(detail, inset above). Sold at an English auction in the late 1980s, the
Cupid plane is now in a private European collection. The miniature has
a convex sole and a ornately shaped iron, designed for creating a
molding pattern on the edge of a concave frame or panel. At left is a
mini boxwood router plane, modeled after a southern German router
plane from the first half of the 17th century. The top of the tool is
carved in the form of a woman's face; the chips come out of her mouth.
A user-made brass ruler lends a sense of scale. The framed relief
carving on the easel in the background, also by Brookshaw, is a
miniature of a mid-17th-century relief-carved scene, probably
Scandinavian or Dutch in origin. The scene features two workmen,
one planing at a bench and the other turning on a spring-pole lathe. A
woman is entering the shop, offering what looks to be a tankard of ale.

Scale tools: Collection of Ronald W. Pearson, D.O.
Cupid plane detail: From the collection of Roger B. Phillips

Mini dividers

This little tool, made by David Brookshaw, is a remarkable miniature of a highly ornate pair of dividers—the original is held in a private European collection. With its legs barely 1 in. long, the dividers is made of cast iron and shows remarkably fine detail.

Collection of Ronald W. Pearson, D.O.

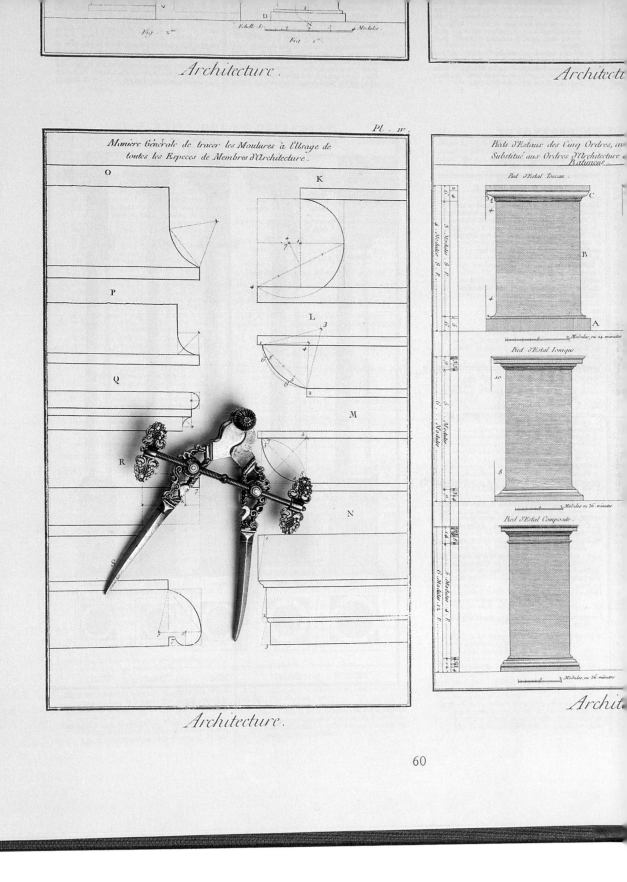

Miniature plane, brace, and marking gauge

These ivory-handled tools were made by Paul Hamler. Each has a body cast from sterling silver. Hamler fabricated the ivory components by cutting up antique ivory billiard cue balls. While the designs of the Miller's Patent plane, Ultimatum-style brace, and ivory marking gauge correspond to their vintage counterparts, none of these miniatures is an exact reproduction. The design of the Ultimatum-style brace (detail, left) is the creation of Paul Hamler; no vintage tool known to exist bears similar engraving (although many collectors dream of finding just such a tool). Starting with a full-size engraving done by English engraver Art Adshell, Hamler took a mold off, then reproduced it in miniature. This was used to cast the brace's quarter plates, with the engraving as part of the mold. Hamler then touched up the engraved lines to get the crisp detail shown here.

Courtesy of Paul Hamler

Tidey Patent plane mini

The Tidey Patent plane, here created in miniature by Paul Hamler, was one of the most complicated planes ever produced. Designed to bevel both edges of a board at once, the plane's two cutters are mounted in separate bodies that may be set to different angles and locked with thumbscrews riding in slots on the curved brass compasses. You can see the complex three-tier hinge reflected in the mirror of the vintage lady's compact that the miniature Tidey sits on. The tool is less than 4½ in. long. Although original Tidey Patent planes were built from other woods (not many were ever made, as it was never a very popular tool), only one ebony Tidey is thought to exist. It was recently sold at auction for a record-breaking $27,000!

Courtesy of Paul Hamler

Petite plow plane

Looking as if it had been left on this clothespin sawhorse by a Lilliputian cabinetmaker, Paul Hamler's miniature model of a Sandusky centerwheel plow plane is only 2¼ in. long. The plane has a rosewood body, boxwood arms, and a fence with ivory trim. All the hardware, brass knurled centerwheel, and knobs are true to scale. Hamler's name is engraved into the upper end of the plane iron.

Courtesy of Paul Hamler

Miniature Miller's Patent plane

A miniature rendition of the coveted No. 50 Miller's Patent plane made by Paul Hamler differs subtly from the bronze No. 50 shown on p. 55. The original plane's copper wash plating was applied on top of cast iron. The process involved first heating the tool and dipping it in hot shellac. The iron was then sprinkled with a potpourri of fine powdered metals ("brown powders"). Hamler says the appearance of the miniature is just a shadow of the original tool's bright finish.

Courtesy of Paul Hamler

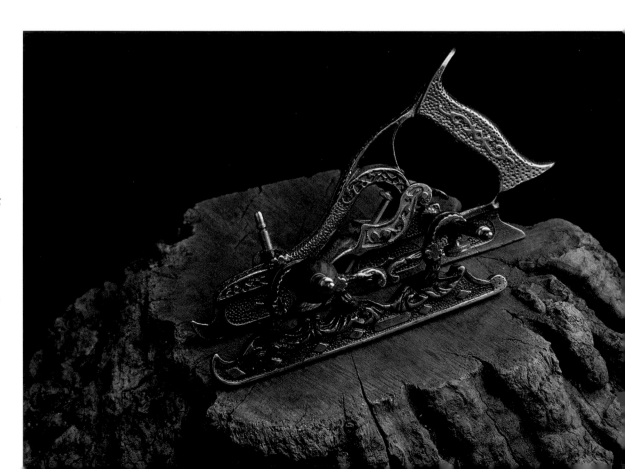

and does tracings or full-size sketches of each part, then uses a photocopier to reduce the parts to ⅓ scale (some larger tools, such as a treadle-powered jigsaw, are done in ⅙ scale). To maintain strict tolerances, he manufactures most of the scale parts—even the wood parts—using precision metalworking equipment, such as milling machines and lathes.

Many tools require cast metal parts, for which Hamler has learned the investment casting process: A wooden or wax model of a part, such as the body and fence of the Miller's Patent #42 plow plane shown in the photo at left, is used to make a mold from which the part is cast in wax. The wax is then "invested," or covered with a thick plaster jacket. The plaster is heated until the wax melts away and evaporates, then the hollow mold is used to cast the part—Hamler typically casts brass, bronze, silver, and gold. Occasionally, he must reproduce an unusual original finish on a miniature, such as the copper wash plating on the Miller's Patent No. 50 plane, shown in the bottom photo on the facing page.

Hamler has also had to make a number of special tools to create certain parts to accurate scale. He built and patented a special miniature screwthread-cutting device, which allows him to make wood threads down to ³⁄₁₆ in. dia., such as used on the centerwheel plow shown in the top photo on the facing page. He also designed a special spring-loaded diamond cutter to perform extra-fine engraving and scrimshaw work using a commercial pantographic carving machine.

Seventeen years ago, Paul Hamler started a woodworking career custom building Chippendale-style furniture. The tool-collection bug bit him as he purchased many vintage hand tools to build his period-style work. When an Ultimatum brace turned out to be beyond his financial reach, he decided to build a ⅓-scale replica. After taking the brace to several tool shows, Hamler found quite a bit of interest in his creation and decided to start making miniatures full time.

To date, Hamler has created accurate and highly detailed miniatures of more than 50 different vintage tools, including the tools shown here and in the photos on pp. 204-209. To satisfy the demand, he makes limited editions of each tool; 100 for basic tools, such as braces, handsaws, and marking gauges. More complex pieces, such as the tiny Tidey Patent plane (see p. 205) are done in editions of 50.

After borrowing a good example of a vintage tool, Hamler dismantles the tool

MINIATURE-LATHE CANE HANDLE

Albert LeCoff, founder of the Wood Turning Center in Philadelphia, Pennsylvania, received a most spectacular birthday gift back in 1989: a collection of 30 canes and walking sticks fashioned by some of the world's prominent turners. The collection included a miniature battery-powered wood lathe by Vermont wood turner Johannes Michelsen. Starting with an ebony spindle for the cane's shaft, Michelsen bored out the top section large enough to hold six AA batteries. These power a 9-volt electric motor fitted into a curly maple and cocobolo housing that serves as the cane's handle. The back end of the housing has a micro-switch that activates the small 18,000-RPM motor, originally designed for model aircraft. The entire motor-housing assembly screws to the cane's shaft with a pair of copper plumbing fixtures. Michelsen's brother made a faceplate for the mini-lathe by turning down a nickel coin, then mounted a rough-turned cocobolo bowl to the tiny faceplate with four #2 screws. At the far end of the ebony shaft, the tip of the cane unscrews (by means of brass air-line fittings from an automotive supply) and becomes a turning tool with a snakewood handle. In the photo below, LeCoff cradles the lathe cane in his lap and takes a scant shaving off the bowl, employing the tool rest Michelsen made from a length of ³⁄₁₆-in.-dia. drill rod.

Rabbit planes

A visual pun worthy of Bugs Bunny, this trio of rabbet planes is a bit of whimsy created by Paul Hamler. The largest bunny, cast from bronze, and the sterling-silver midsize rabbit are both working planes, each fitted with tiny irons and wedges. The smallest silver bunny is a lady's pendant.

Courtesy of Paul Hamler

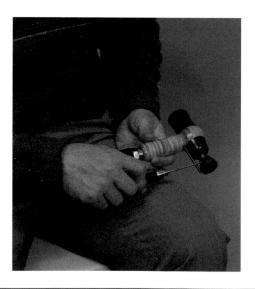

This miniature working lathe is contained in the handle of a very special cane, constructed by Johannes Michelsen for Albert LeCoff, founder of the Wood Turning Center in Philadelphia.

Mini pedal jigsaw

Paul Hamler's miniature machine is a ⅙-scale Barnes velocipede No. 2 scrollsaw, originally manufactured in the late 19th and early 20th centuries. Made of cast bronze and curly maple, the working model accurately echoes the original's tractor-like seat, 7-in. narrow blade, and 24-in.-deep throat.

Courtesy of Lee Valley Tools

Ultimatum brace with miniature

The classic brass and ebony Hibernia Ultimatum brace, made by Marples and Sons, of Sheffield, England, looms behind a miniature version made by Paul Hamler. Hamler used ebony for the tool's grips to match the original. The Ultimatum-type metallic-framed braces were made by Marples with many different woods used for the infills and grips (see pp. 86-87).

Courtesy of Eric M. Peterson

Mini brass Stanley

The ⅓-scale miniature of a Stanley No. 4½ bench plane was made by Gordon Auld, a Portland, Oregon, artisan, mechanic, and tool collector. Machined from solid brass stock and fitted with rosewood handles, the miniature is seen in front of a full-sized gunmetal Stanley No. 5.

Courtesy of Darrell Six

Sandusky plow-plane reproductions

The three planes shown here are all copies of the remarkable Sandusky centerwheel plow plane (the original is shown on p. 44). Crafted by Gordon Auld, each of these planes is done in a different scale, from full scale to ½ scale and ⅓ scale. The two larger models have ebony bodies; the smallest is rosewood. All have ivory tips.

Courtesy of Darrell Six and Steven F. Dice

THE ART OF THE TOOL, AND TOOLS AS ART

We usually think of tools as implements that help us to realize the products of our inspiration: to take a material such as wood and make it into chairs, canoes, or cottages; barns, bridges, or balusters. But sometimes, these implements, which need only be utilitarian, become themselves the products of human inspiration. You can construct a simple, functional ruler by incising a series of measured, parallel marks onto a strip of wood or metal. But if you take the time to engrave a few curlicues or add a geometric pattern that decorates the space between the inch marks, you can create an artistic tool. An artistic ruler is no more or less useful than an unadorned ruler, but it can be more pleasurable to use. Just as a bit of paint, an attractive set of curtains, and a few paintings and posters can turn a sterile room into a warm and cozy living space, so too does the human spirit benefit from a little extra attention paid to aesthetic details.

Few people would think of examining a woodworking tool such as a handplane or a bit brace the way one might evaluate a stylish Italian sports car, in terms of the proportions of its form or the sinuousness of its lines. But some tools have more graceful forms than others, and their grace makes them even more appealing. Often a tool's beauty may drive woodworkers and collectors alike to scour flea markets and junk shops in search of new treasures for their toolboxes or display cabinets.

The overall shape of a tool and the way it is ornamented usually reflect the trends and styles of its time of creation. For example, look at the ornate detail lavished upon tools produced in the Victorian era, such as the Miller's Patent combination plane in the bottom photo on p. 218. Another example, from a different design era, is the streamlined form of the Millers Falls handplanes in the top photo on p. 218, which clearly embody the tenets of Art Deco; the tools look as if they could jump off your workbench and set a land speed record!

The elements that make a tool special and desirable aren't always visual. Tools must be held to be used, and the way a tool appeals to the touch is another type of aesthetic sensation. Every craftsman has had the experience of picking up a tool and lighting up inside with immense satisfaction: The tool just *feels* right. Although the word "ergonomic" wasn't even coined when many of the implements in this book were made, the makers often designed their tools with handles that precisely fit both the hand of the user and the style of the tool.

Having the right "feel" involves not only the shape of the grip or handle itself, but also its material, texture, and placement, which affect the balance of the entire tool. A tool that feels good is a delight to hold and a pleasure to use, and it can make tedious work go by more quickly. And when it's time to call it a day, such a tool doesn't continue to remind the user of the day's efforts—it doesn't leave the craftsman with a hand full of blisters!

So far, I have been discussing the artistic properties that decorative tools possess. But when the aesthetic form of a tool takes precedence over its function, it jumps the boundaries of a woodworking tool and becomes a piece of artwork, or what I like to call "functional sculpture." Made more for the display case than the tool chest, such "fantasy" tools may not be ready for a day's toil, but are nevertheless inspiring to behold. (In fact, photographing the remarkable tools for this book inspired me to get creative and build the "biplane" handplane, shown in the top photo on p. 228.) The usefulness of such tools usually takes a back seat to their artistry. It's hard to imagine the French reclining woman plane, shown at right and in the photo on p. 227, being used to take more than a few quick shavings. (Apparently this impression wasn't shared by many old-time craftsmen, as some of the most imaginative tools show ample signs of wear.)

At the end of this chapter there are a few examples of objects whose forms were inspired by woodworking tools. These items really could be part of their own book of objects d'art. But I've included them to help complete the story of the art of fine tools. They serve as a reminder that the world of woodworking tools carries with it powerful imagery: of colorful traditions of building that are long gone; of the charm of the solitary craftsman creating lovely and useful objects; of the joy and romance of handling and working with beautiful, sweet-smelling wood. Finally, we are reminded of the power and magic of woodworking tools themselves, and the pleasure that an excellent tool can bring to the hands—and aesthetic senses—of the user. ✶

English turnscrews

Metal screws came into common use in woodworking in the late 18th century, and so did the tools to drive them. The tray of this tool chest contains a small collection of early turnscrews, or English pattern screwdrivers. Most of these were made by blacksmiths or the craftsmen who used them. Turnscrews were often made from recycled metal; an old worn, file would be ground into a shapely tool that could serve a second useful life.

From the collection of Bill Phillips

Coachmaker's rabbet planes

A matched pair of left-hand and right-hand tools, these coachmaker's planes are made from Macassar ebony and brass, with steel cutters. The short skate and fence (seen at the midsection of each tool) allowed it to follow a curved surface and to work in tight spaces. Craftsmen building stylish coaches and carriages used these planes to plow grooves in the curved frames for fitting panels and upholstery. A long, curved brass wedge holds the cutter in place; both follow the graceful form of the tool's body.

From the collection of Roger B. Phillips

Challenge plane

The novel form of the Challenge jack plane's iron body combines the function of frog, wedge, and adjustment mechanism in its arched blade holder. The tool's unique design was not understated in a seller's ad, which reads: "We offer in the Challenge planes the utmost simplicity of construction in a perfect woodworking tool." Patented by Arthur Goldsborough in 1883 and manufactured for only a brief time, the Challenge plane is an example of an interesting design that failed to be competitive with planes produced by major tools companies of the era, most notably the Stanley Rule & Level Company.

From the collection of Steve Johnson

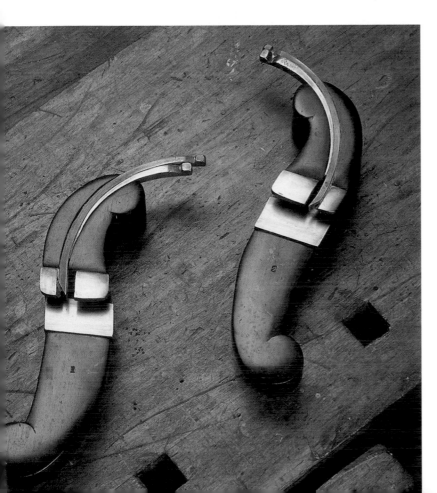

215

American smooth plane

The graceful shape of this Knowles-type smooth plane and the fanciful outline of its cast-iron body are classic and timeless. The plane, c. 1825-1850, is thought to have been manufactured in the United States by a European immigrant.

From the collection of John and Janet Wells

Iron shoulder plane

This shoulder plane, of unknown manufacture, has a graceful, sculpturally shaped iron body (which has been skillfully repaired). The heavy body was cast in two halves in order to create a hollow in the center for the plane iron to pass through. The halves are held together by pins.

Collection of Ronald W. Pearson, D.O.

Sargent ladybug plane

The Sargent No. 1507½ iron bullnose plane at right has a unique profile that eventually inspired the nickname of "ladybug." Sargent & Company of New Haven, Connecticut, was a fierce competitor of the Stanley Rule & Level Company. By the late 19th century, Sargent manufactured equivalents for practically the entire Stanley line, including more than 100 different types and sizes of handplanes and scrapers, not to mention a few that Stanley didn't offer.

From the collection of Clifford R. Sapienza

Birmingham plane

Manufactured by the Birmingham Plane Company, of Shelton, Connecticut, in about 1890, this 6⁷⁄₁₆-in.-long smooth plane is all metal: The sole, bed, and handles are part of a single, elegantly shaped casting. A small lever just behind the blade assembly adjusts the position of the plane's 1½-in.-wide iron.

From the collection of George Gaspari

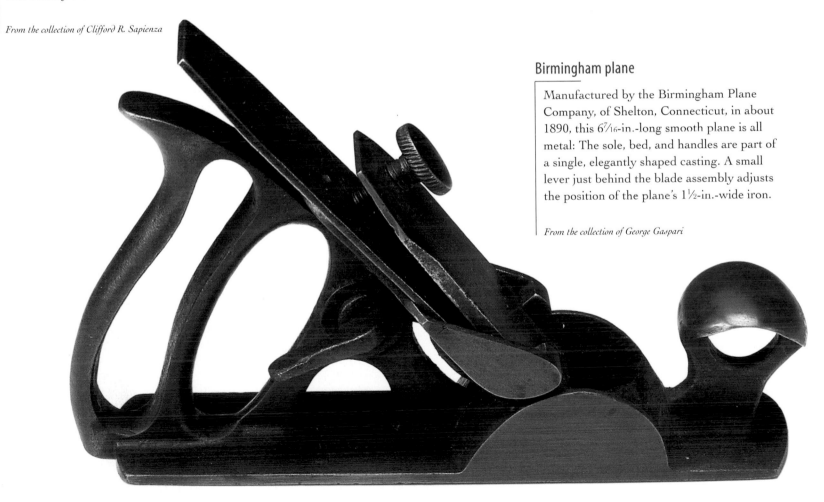

Did you know that the same post-World-War-II movement in industrial design that gave the world remarkable streamlined creations such as the Chrysler Air Flow car and the Flying Zephyr railroad locomotive also inspired a line of woodworking tools? Influenced heavily by the Art Deco period Streamline Moderne design style, tool manufacturer Millers Falls developed a line of hand tools that the company produced from 1949 though the mid-1950s (it is speculated that the actual designs were penned by one of the leading industrial design houses of the time).

The Streamline Moderne line included these tools from the collection of Clifford R. Sapienza: from left to right, the No. 100A automatic push drill, the No. 714 jack plane, the No. 709 smooth plane, and the No. 104 geared hand drill (a hacksaw was also part of the line). All of the tools share streamlined forms, aluminum or gray-enameled cast-iron construction, chrome-plated components, and, most notably, handles made from glossy red Tenite plastic. The handplanes in particular have elegant streamlined shapes that are futuristic enough to have earned them the nickname of "Buck Rogers" handplanes. The eye-catching good looks of the entire line no doubt helped to make these tools very popular, as they remain with woodworkers and collectors today.

Miller's Patent humpback plane

The floral motifs and hollow scallop shell in the ornate casting of this Stanley first model No. 41 Miller's Patent combination plane are indicative of the Victorian era it was made in. Among collectors, this plane is known as "the hook" or "the humpback" because of its bulging upper body and small recurving tab—a small but significant detail.

From the collection of John and Janet Wells

Boston Metallic plane

A rather minimalist approach was take in the design of this 11-in.-long T-rabbet plane, manufactured by the Boston Metallic Plane Co. in about 1875. A single cast-iron arch supports the front portion of the sole while providing abundant side clearance (important when working in tight quarters) as well as clearance for chips. One nice touch is the tab in the casting at the base of the arch, which provides a stop for the rosewood wedge that holds the blade in place.

From the collection of
Clifford R. Sapienza

Birmingham shoulder rabbet plane

The small cast "batwing" detail just above and behind the blade is a distinguishing characteristic of the larger-sized Birmingham Plane Co. T-rabbet coachmaker's planes. While the detail on the one-piece cast-iron plane has no functional purpose, it's just the kind of delightful little decoration so sorely missing on most contemporary woodworking tools.

Courtesy of Jon Zimmers

Ergonomic planes

Both these planes have gracefully shaped bodies and handles that allow the user good control of the tool. The patternmaker's plane at far right has a curved mahogany handle that fits the hand comfortably and transfers power fluidly to the convex sole. (The sole, incidentally, is removable and may be exchanged for other radius sole and cutter sets, making the plane more versatile.) The bronze-bodied compass plane to its left is a one-of-a-kind tool, probably made by a patternmaker. The shape of the tool's flexible steel sole can be adjusted for a convex or concave cut by means of a unique lever.

From the collection of Clifford R. Sapienza

Handrailer's squirrel-tail plane

The Macassar ebony handle on this handrailer's plane is most comfortable for the hand and resembles a squirrel's tail. The short convex sole of this plane was designed for shaping curved handrails. The decorative dot inlaid into the handle is ivory.

From the collection of Clifford R. Sapienza

A look at early planes will convince you that their makers knew little about ergonomics; the only way to use most of these tools was to grasp the body and push. But over the centuries, callus-weary craftsmen have adapted the shapes of their planes to make them more comfortable to use.

In the photo below are five variations on the design of a horn plane's front grip that demonstrate different approaches innovative craftsmen have taken. At far left, a simple rounded handle, quickly shaped by its maker to final contour with a rasp (note the tool marks still in the blond wood) and joined to the body with a single large dovetail. Second from left: an older European grip, sawn from flat cherry stock and sculpted with a slight scroll at the top. This grip is glued and nailed into a slot in the front of the plane. At center: a hornbeam grip in the shape of a carver's mallet on a European smooth plane, conventionally turned on a lathe, then doweled into a semicircular base at the front. Second from right: This plane's horn is a horn—the grip was made from the tip of a small cow horn screwed to the front of the wood-bodied scrub plane (is this how the front grip of these handplanes got their name in the first place?). At far right: a popular European-style grip, carved from a piece of burl walnut shaped to suit the user's grip and fastened via a shallow mortise to the front of a smooth plane. The upsweeping curve of the grip shows that it was made for a right-handed user.

The planes shown in the photo are from the collection of Steven F. Dice.

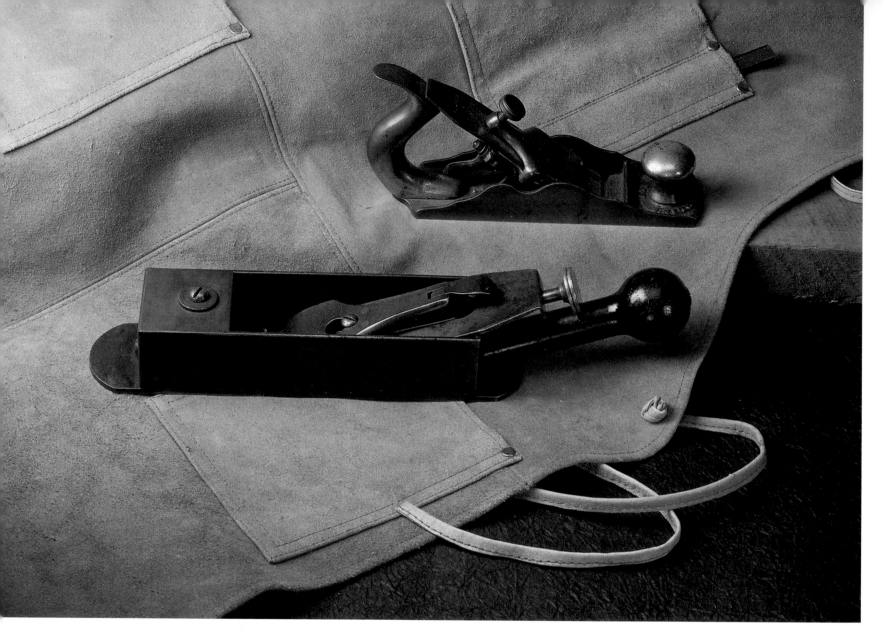

Chaplin and Bailey low-angle planes

Both of these planes have smooth-cutting, low-angle blades, and
unusual handles that make them more user friendly. On the
O. R. Chaplin's Patent No. 1 smooth plane (in the background), the
curvaceous handle protrudes beyond the rear end of its 7-in.-long sole,
providing clearance from the iron and adjustment lever. In front of
the Chaplin is a cabinetmaker's block plane made by L. Bailey &
Company, of Boston. To provide a comfortable grip behind the iron,
the Bailey has a long "broomstick" handle. This design was patented by
Leonard Bailey in 1858 and later produced by The Stanley Rule &
Level Company as its popular No. 9 (see the facing page).

From the collection of George Gaspari

Stanley No. 9 block plane

In addition to its rear knob, this Stanley No. 9 block plane has a removable handle, commonly called a "hot dog" by collectors. The hollow cast-iron handle can be mounted on either side of the plane as needed for right-hand or left-handed operation. The long block plane, made from 1870 through 1943, has sides that are ground flat and square with the bottom, so it works superbly with a shooting board.

Courtesy of Jon Zimmers

Dolphin plane front handle

Perhaps to bring good luck, the Scottish boat builder who made this plane, known as the Anstruther plane (see p. 166), carved its horn in the form of a mythical dolphin. Lest you think it a better fish sculpture than a handle, the horn shows ample signs of wear, indicating that the plane saw a long and useful life in the workshop.

From the collection of Roger B. Phillips

Scottish miter plane with ram's horn grip

This small miter plane was probably made in the mid-1800s. The rectangular metal body with wood infills was pretty much standard for such planes by the end of the 18th century. The scroll-carved front grip is common for this period and similar to grips on wood-bodied continental planes made in earlier periods. The plane body is wrought iron, which is more resistant to rusting than the mild steel often seen in woodworking tools today. The plane has a very small mouth opening, set by a two-piece iron sole joined to the sides with dovetails.

From the collection of John and Janet Wells

Fiddlehead plow plane

You might guess from the carved scroll handle on this ash plow plane that it was made for violinmaking...but you'd be wrong! No doubt inspired by the headstock scroll carved on all violins and fiddles, the plane was designed for the coachmaking trade. The plane's short sole and skate and convex-curved-faced fence allowed it to plow curved or circular grooves and rabbets.

From the collection of Steven F. Dice

TOOLS OF FACT AND FANTASY:
THE ART OF DAVID BROOKSHAW

In the fine arts, such as sculpture and painting, artists usually begin with a lump of clay or a blank canvas before applying their imagination and energy toward the creation of a piece. In a practical field such as toolmaking, using the basic form of an implement such as a plane, saw, or brace as the foundation for creative expression is unusual, and may seem radical and contemporary. But there does exist a limited tradition that European craftsman have embraced for centuries, resulting in rare and wonderful tools that were possibly made as gifts for nobility or kings. Such tools are as much sculpture as they are implements of woodworking. They may tell a story with the actual characters represented (see the Don Quixote hand adze on p. 116) or simply render a vision of fantasy from the mind of the creator.

Today, the tradition of fantasy tools is carried on by English toolmaker and miniaturist David Brookshaw. The five boxwood tools pictured here, from the collection of Roger B. Phillips, represent two aspects of Brookshaw's art: his ability to reproduce historical tools (usually as scale models) and his genius for creating his own original "tool sculptures."

The 3½-in.-long horse plane at far left is modeled after an existing historical piece from a European collection. The brace with the carved face is Brookshaw's interpretation of similar period braces, such as the brace shown on p. 174. The brace shown above is about 6½ in. long and has an ivory ring and a button on the grip.

The 1½-in.-long duck plane in the foreground is built like a small rabbet plane. The end of its wedge is carved in the form of a fledgling chick riding atop its mama's back. The router plane at back right is carved in the figure of a *koi* (a Japanese carp). In use, the plane's ³⁄₁₆-in.-wide cutter sends shavings out of the fish's mouth. The 7-in.-long plane at front right also makes use of the *koi* motif, with the carved carp serving as a front grip.

Ebony plane

A dark theme pervades this ½-scale model of a French plane
from the 19th century, rendered by English toolmaker
David Brookshaw. Measuring 9½ in. in length, the black
ebony plane's body portrays a reclining female nude on a
platform, which conveniently serves as the plane's narrow
sole. The plane's handle is skillfully carved in the form of
a demon-faced apparition that hovers over the woman,
seemingly with ill intent.

Collection of Ronald W. Pearson, D.O.

Biplane plane

Having fun with a pun, the author created this small wood plane in the form of a biplane. The body, wings, and tail are all fabricated from purpleheart, while the struts, propeller, and wedge (shaped into the form of a leather-helmeted pilot) are made from narrah. The 9-in.-long plane with its 1¼-in.-wide blade works quite well as a smooth plane, although holding it takes a bit of getting used to. Unfortunately, the propeller doesn't spin while you are taking a shaving.

From the collection of the author

Carpenter's plane toolbox

What more appropriate symbol could a carpenter's union choose than a jointer plane? Carpenter's Union No. 3 of Wheeling, West Virginia, made this 2½-ft.-long plane to identify the unit when its members marched in town parades (a hole in the bottom of the plane accepts a wooden pole). The top of the plane is hollow so it can serve as a tool caddy (or perhaps tote a supply of refreshments to the parade). Alas, it is said that Union #3 had to sell its parade plane after an unscrupulous treasurer embezzled funds, leaving the union bankrupt.

From the collection of Steven F. Dice

Snail and aardvark planes

Here are a couple of the strangest planes ever, made as birthday gifts by Bellingham, Washington, toolmaker Michael Flaherty. The snail plane's body is carved from jet black Gabon ebony, with the antennae fabricated from brass rod. A carved rosewood spiral shell makes up the rear handle of this plane, which is fully functional. The aardvark plane was carved from a block of osage orange.

From the collection of Valdis Petersons

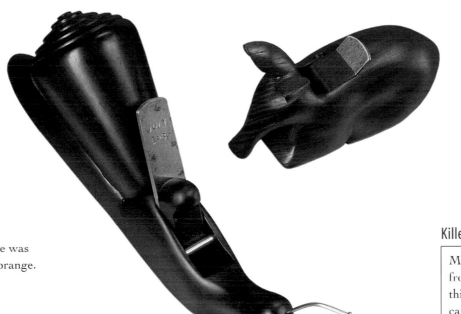

Killer-whale block plane

Made by David Brookshaw from ebony with ivory inlays, this 4½-in.-long block plane is carved in the form of a killer whale. The cleverly designed plane uses the top dorsal fin as a wedge to secure the T-shaped iron (which is narrow at the top and widens to ¾ in. at the business end). The light-colored underside of the whale is an inlaid section of ivory, which makes a durable sole.

From the collection of Roger B. Phillips

Trench-art coin-bank plane

Many of the Allied soldiers of World War I had a grim lot: to fight and die in the muddy trenches of Western Europe. To pass the time (and relieve the tedium), some soldiers fabricated souvenirs for friends and their loved ones back home. Known collectively as "trench art," pieces such as boxes, banks, picture frames, and vases were made from whatever materials were on hand. This novel coin bank in the shape of a wooden horn plane was made in Calais, France, and brought home by a lucky G.I. The top and false blade swivel sideways, allowing coins to be deposited (detail, above). On one side are carved crossed cavalry swords; on the other, the dates 1914 and 1919 (the start and end of World War I) and the words "World War." (At the time, no one suspected there would be a second world war about two decades later.)

From the collection of Steven F. Dice

Shrine woodworking

Made by the author in 1989 for an employees' art exhibit at The
Taunton Press, this piece was inspired by Taoist shrines found in
homes throughout Asia. The shrine is made from mahogany, with
candles fabricated from bench chisels with engine-turned and polished
circular sawblades with electric lights mounted on them. The
craftsman's poem by St. Francis is flanked by measuring tapes set into
fluted columns. On top are a cornice with dovetail dentil molding,
plate-joinery biscuits, a small plane (a pencil sharpener, actually), and
router-bit finials. A glass offerings dish full of rosewood shavings is
inset into the shelf, which is edged with grooved dowels. An homage to
woodworking tools and fine craftsmanship, this mixed-media creation
is a fitting tribute to the spirit of this book.

PUBLISHER: Jim Childs

ASSOCIATE PUBLISHER: Helen Albert

ASSOCIATE EDITOR: Strother Purdy

DESIGNER/LAYOUT ARTIST: Mary Terrizzi

EDITOR: Ruth Dobsevage

TYPEFACE: Cochin

PAPER: Warren Patina, 70 lb.

PRINTER: R. R. Donnelley, Willard, Ohio

Shrine woodworking

Made by the author in 1989 for an employees' art exhibit at The Taunton Press, this piece was inspired by Taoist shrines found in homes throughout Asia. The shrine is made from mahogany, with candles fabricated from bench chisels with engine-turned and polished circular sawblades with electric lights mounted on them. The craftsman's poem by St. Francis is flanked by measuring tapes set into fluted columns. On top are a cornice with dovetail dentil molding, plate-joinery biscuits, a small plane (a pencil sharpener, actually), and router-bit finials. A glass offerings dish full of rosewood shavings is inset into the shelf, which is edged with grooved dowels. An homage to woodworking tools and fine craftsmanship, this mixed-media creation is a fitting tribute to the spirit of this book.

PUBLISHER: Jim Childs

ASSOCIATE PUBLISHER: Helen Albert

ASSOCIATE EDITOR: Strother Purdy

DESIGNER/LAYOUT ARTIST: Mary Terrizzi

EDITOR: Ruth Dobsevage

TYPEFACE: Cochin

PAPER: Warren Patina, 70 lb.

PRINTER: R. R. Donnelley, Willard, Ohio